STUDENT'S BOOK

English Explorer 4

Helen Stephenson

NATIONAL GEOGRAPHIC LEARNING | CENGAGE Learning

Australia • Brazil • Japan • Korea • Mexico • Singapore • Spain • United Kingdom • United States

Contents

Skills: Listening & Speaking	Working with words Study skills Pronunciation	Culture & CLIL
Listening: Conversations about TV shows **Speaking:** Exchanging opinions	**Working with words:** verb + preposition *at, to*; noun + noun **Study skills:** identifying the main idea in a text **Pronunciation:** words ending in *-ght* and *-ghed*	**Reading:** New Zealand on film **Listening:** A conversation about film locations **CLIL:** Social science and English Media studies
Listening: A podcast about phobias **Speaking:** Checking information	**Working with words:** abstract nouns; verb + *-ing* **Study skills:** making notes **Pronunciation:** intonation in question tags	**Reading:** Irish traditions **Listening:** A survey about beliefs **CLIL:** Biology and English Animals and people
Listening: Recipe instructions **Speaking:** Talking about quantity, time, distance, etc.	**Working with words:** verb + *to* + infinitive; American English **Study skills:** listening for key words **Pronunciation:** words containing *ui*	**Reading:** American food **Listening:** Meal-time conversations **CLIL:** Maths and English The history of numbers
Listening: A conversation about clothes **Speaking:** Talking about preferences	**Working with words:** adjective + *to* + infinitive; verb + noun combinations **Study skills:** mind maps **Pronunciation:** words with /s/ and /z/ sounds	**Reading:** Sport in Australia **Listening:** Sports news **CLIL:** Physics and English Newton's law of motion
Listening: A story from Greek mythology **Speaking:** Expressing purpose and giving reasons	**Working with words:** adjective order; verb + preposition **Study skills:** scanning and skimming **Pronunciation:** the letter 'o' and the vowel sounds /əʊ/ and /ʌ/	**Reading:** Boom-town Canada **Listening:** Statistics about Canada **CLIL:** Chemistry and English Elements
Listening: A radio programme about an art forgery **Speaking:** Making and responding to requests	**Working with words:** phrasal verbs; noun + preposition combinations **Study skills:** answering questions **Pronunciation:** words containing *au*	**Reading:** British best-sellers **Listening:** A radio programme about women authors **CLIL:** Art and English Leonardo da Vinci
Listening: Comments about four famous people **Speaking:** Talking about regrets and making criticisms	**Working with words:** prefixes; suffixes **Study skills:** dictionary skills **Pronunciation:** silent letters	**Reading:** South African life **Listening:** A tour of Cape Town **CLIL:** History and English The human journey
Listening: A shopping questionnaire **Speaking:** Returning things to shops	**Working with words:** reporting verbs; word combinations with *money* **Study skills:** listening and checking **Pronunciation:** syllable stress	**Reading:** Shopping online in the UK **Listening:** A telephone conversation following an online purchase **CLIL:** Maths and English Statistics

Starter

1 Match the descriptions (1–4) with the people in the photo (a–d).

1 Fay has got long dark hair. She's wearing a red jacket.
2 Dan has got short black hair. His top is white and red.
3 Holly has got fair hair in a ponytail. She's wearing a white top and jeans.
4 Joe is tall and he's got short dark hair. He's wearing jeans and white trainers.

2 S.1 **Read and listen to the dialogue. Complete each sentence with the correct name.**

1 .... has just been to the shops.
2 .... has changed his/her appearance.
3 .... went camping in Scotland.
4 .... is going to study at lunchtime.

3 Read the dialogue again. Who is interested in each of these things?

acting animals clothes photography

4 Write sentences about these things. They can be true or false. Exchange your sentences with a partner. Find your partner's false sentences.

- places you've been to recently
- things you did in the summer holidays
- things you're going to do this term

Dan: Hi, Fay! Hi, Holly!
Holly: Hi, Dan! Are you ready for tomorrow?
Dan: Oh, don't remind me. I hate the first day back at school. But I've bought some great new trainers – what do you think?
Holly: Cool!
Fay: Hey, Dan, have you heard from Joe? Is he back from Australia?
Dan: Yes, he is. In fact, look! Here he comes.
Fay: Oh, yes … he looks different. Is he thinner?
Holly: No, I think he's changed his hairstyle.
Joe: Hi, everyone!
Fay: Hi, Joe! What was Australia like?
Joe: It was cold – it's winter there now, you know! But it was brilliant. I took thousands of photos. What about you? Have you had a good summer?
Fay: Yeah, it's been OK.
Holly: I went camping on the west coast of Scotland.
Dan: Oh, I've been there. It's nice but a bit boring.
Holly: Well, OK, there aren't a lot of clothes shops, Dan, but I joined this wildlife group – they were doing a survey on dolphins. I was thinking about …
Joe: Don't tell me! You're going to start a new wildlife club at school this year.
Holly: Well, why not? What are you going to do?
Joe: Hmm, I'm not going to miss any deadlines, that's for sure! Last year was a disaster.
Fay: I know! I'm going to do all my homework at lunchtime – I need to be free after school for the drama group.
Holly: Anyway, Joe. You look …
Joe: Taller? I've grown eight centimetres this summer! I'm as tall as my dad now.
Fay: No way!

1 Fame

> Grammar

Review the present simple, present continuous, and the present perfect simple.

Review *yet, still, already* and *just.*

> Vocabulary

Learn words connected with mass media and TV shows.

Work with verb + preposition *at* and *to* combinations, and noun + noun combinations.

> Skills

Read about a reality show's secret house, Cheryl Cole's career, and New Zealand on film.

Listen to conversations about TV shows, and a conversation about film locations.

Write a review.

> Communicate

Exchange opinions.

1 **What do you think is happening in the photo?**

2 **Work in pairs. Connect the words in the vocabulary box to these words. How many connections can you make?**

TV	newspapers and magazines
radio	the Internet

article audience channel front page headline journalist listener podcast programme reader reporter station video-sharing viewer website

3 **Ask and answer questions about the media.**

1. How many hours a week do you watch TV?
2. Which radio programmes do you like?
3. What is the best way to follow the news?
4. Which magazines do you read?

4 1.1 **Listen to a survey about the media. What answers does the person give?**

1A Fans

'SECRET' HOUSE – NOW NOT SO SECRET!

Our reporter investigates.

In a quiet, residential street in north London, a group of teenagers is standing opposite a large house. They are staring at the windows of the first floor. They can't see much because they're on the other side of the street and a high wall surrounds the house. There are several security guards at the gate and a policeman in the street. This is the *X Factor* house – the contestants are staying here during the competition. In theory, the location of the house is a secret. However, *X Factor* fans have discovered its address.

Chloe, Sharon and Hayley come here every day. The schools are on holiday this week. 'We're waiting to talk to Olly. I've brought my autograph book with me and Sharon has borrowed her mum's camera. It's like a paparazzi camera, with a long lens,' Hayley explains to me. She's showing me her autograph book so that I can look at some of the signed photos – she's met almost everyone on TV! Sharon is pointing the camera at the house. An older girl, Tara, is waving to the group from the house next door. Tara says it's the first time a celebrity has lived in her street. She thinks it's 'really cool', although many of the neighbours have complained.

I've never seen the show, so I ask the girls about the contestants. 'They all sing really well, but Olly's definitely got the *X Factor*!' says Sharon. Chloe, Sharon and Hayley vote for him every week and they watch repeats of the show on *YouTube*. It's time for my last question. 'Have you ever spoken to any of your idols?' 'No, we haven't, but we're not giving up!'

Speaking

1 **Work in pairs. Who or what are you a fan of? Tell your partner. Give reasons.**

an actor   an author   a sports star
a sports team   a pop star   a TV show

I'm Jackie Chan's biggest fan. I think he's …

I'm crazy about Leona Lewis because …

Reading and listening

2 **Read the news story quickly. What is it about?**

3 1.2 **Read and listen to the news story. Are the sentences true or false?**

1 Chloe, Sharon and Hayley live in the *X Factor* house.
2 They are waiting to speak to one of the *X Factor* contestants.
3 Tara doesn't like living next door to the house.
4 The girls talk to the contestants every day.

Grammar: the present simple, continuous and perfect

4 **Look at the examples (1–4). Match them with the meanings (a–d).**

1 A group of teenagers is standing opposite a large house.
2 A high wall surrounds the house.
3 The contestants are staying here during the competition.
4 Chloe, Sharon and Hayley come here every day.

a a permanent state
b an activity in progress now
c an activity in progress around now
d a regular activity

See Grammar Explorer: Page 116

5 **Write the correct form of the verbs: present simple or present continuous.**

Some fans (**1**) .... (**become**) obsessed with their idols. Roger, aged 36, (**2**) .... (**love**) Elvis. He (**3**) .... (**dress**) like Elvis and he's got the same hairstyle. He (**4**) .... (**not sing**) very well, so now he (**5**) .... (**take**) singing lessons as well. Roger's two children are mad about *Star Trek*. They (**6**) .... (**pretend**) to speak Klingon with each other! They (**7**) .... (**go**) to the *Star Trek* convention every year. They (**8**) .... (**save**) their money to go to next year's convention.

6 **Look at the examples (1–4). Match them with the meanings (a–b).**

1 I've brought my autograph book with me.
2 *X Factor* fans have discovered its address.
3 Many of the neighbours have complained.
4 Sharon has borrowed her mum's camera.

a an action in the past with a result in the present
b a past action in a time period which includes the present

See Grammar Explorer: Page 116

We use the present perfect with the expression *It's the first / second / third time.*

7 **Write the correct form of the verbs: present simple, present continuous or present perfect.**

Dan is a member of Keira Knightley's fan club. It's the first time he (**1**) .... (**join**) a fan club and he's really happy because he (**2**) .... (**receive**) a signed poster of Keira. He (**3**) .... (**put**) it on his wall. He (**4**) .... (**stare**) at it every evening. Dan (**5**) .... (**check**) the fan club site most days. Sometimes he (**6**) .... (**spend**) a lot of time online and he (**7**) .... (**not finish**) his homework. Keira (**8**) .... (**make**) a new film at the moment, and there are photos and stories about her every day.

Working with words: verb + preposition *at* and *to*

8 **Look at the examples. Then find five more verbs with *at* and *to* in the text.**

They are staring at the windows.

We're waiting to talk to Olly.

See Working with words: Page 100

Speaking

9 **Write a question for each picture. Use the present perfect form of the verbs.**

1 ever / meet / your idol?

2 ever / watch / your favourite team?

3 ever / join / a fan club?

4 ever / vote for / your idol?

You can use *ever* and *never* with the present perfect when referring to experiences in your life.

10 **Work in pairs. Write a questionnaire to find out who is the biggest fan in your class. Use ideas from the box and Exercise 9. Use the present simple and present perfect forms of the verbs.**

buy	CDs / magazines / books
collect	autographs / posters / photos
copy	a hairstyle / a look / clothes
go to	concerts / matches / shows
queue all night for	a ticket / a book / a seat
spend too much on	DVDs / phone voting / trips to see your idol

11 **Work in pairs. Ask and answer your questions from Exercise 10. Then work with a new partner. Compare the answers with your original partner.**

A: *Have you ever voted for your idol?*
B: *Yes, I have. / No, I haven't.*

Fast finishers

Make a list of all the past participles you can think of in one minute. Then make sentences with them.

1B Reality TV

A

And now, celebrity reality TV!

Are television viewers getting bored with shows like *Survivor* or *You Can Dance*? Maybe ordinary contestants aren't interesting enough – because ITV's new show is called *I'm a Celebrity … Get Me Out Of Here!* Eight celebrities live in the jungle for two weeks while viewers at home vote for their favourite. Although ITV hasn't revealed who the stars are yet, there are lots of rumours. You can see the first episode in August.

B

NEW AWARDS FOR REALITY TV

Reality TV shows have exploded onto our screens in the last couple of years and they have already become extremely popular. So it's not surprising that the Academy of Television Arts and Sciences has just announced a new Emmy award for reality TV. *American Idol* and *Survivor* are both nominated. The Academy considers that reality TV has become a major part of television culture. Perhaps this is true – apparently one in seven UK teenagers wants to become famous through reality TV.

Speaking

1 Work in pairs. Put the words into three groups: *people*, *performance* and *programmes*.

act actor audition celebrity
contestant episode judge presenter
rehearsal series winner

2 Tell your partner about a TV show you like. Use some of the words in the box.

Listening

3 1.3 **Listen to the conversations (1–3) and match them with the TV shows. There is one extra TV show.**

a celebrity show a comedy series
a soap opera a talent show

4 1.3 **Listen again and put the words in the vocabulary box in the order you hear them.**

Reading and listening

5 Quickly read the four news stories (A–D) which appeared over a ten-year period. Which TV programmes are mentioned?

6 1.4 **Read and listen to the news stories (A–D) and match the information (1–4) .**

1 On this show, the audience at home chooses the winner.
2 This show begins with 16 contestants.
3 This programme is ten years old.
4 Reality TV is very popular.

C

A GREAT NEW SHOW

Have you heard about the new TV show yet?

It's called *You Can Dance* and it's all about … dancing! It's a talent competition open to 18–30 year olds. The first stage, the auditions, has already finished. The series starts next week, but the judges are still choosing the final 16 for the first programme. So if you like salsa, hip-hop and jazz, don't miss it!

D

Bye bye Big Brother

Channel 4 has cancelled the next series of *Big Brother*, after ten years of shows. The TV channel hasn't given any reasons for the decision. It still broadcasts *Celebrity Big Brother*, although recently this hasn't been as popular as newer shows such as *I'm a Celebrity … Get Me Out Of Here!* So if you have been on Mars for ten years and you still haven't seen *Big Brother*, the current series is your last chance!

7 **Which is the correct order for the news stories?**

a A B D C
b C D B A
c C B A D

Working with words: noun + noun

8 **Look at the examples. How many nouns can you think of which can follow *television*?**

news + story = news story
talent + competition = talent competition

See Working with words: Page 100

Grammar: *yet, still, already* and *just*

9 **Find *yet, still, already* and *just* in the news stories. Complete the sentences.**

1. We can use .... with the present simple, continuous and negative present perfect.
2. We can use .... in present perfect affirmative sentences.
3. We can use .... in negative sentences and questions.
4. We use .... + present perfect to mean 'a short time ago'.

See Grammar Explorer: Page 117

10 **Mark the correct position of the words.**

e.g. I ^ haven't seen that show. (**still**)

1. Hurry up! The show has started. (**already**)
2. Has the voting finished? (**yet**)
3. The phone lines have closed. (**just**)
4. The judges are discussing the performance. (**still**)
5. They haven't announced the results. (**yet**)

11 **Make statements and questions with the words.**

e.g. the presenter / not rehearse / yet
The presenter hasn't rehearsed yet.

1. the rehearsals / finish / already
2. the audience / come in / just
3. the judges / sit down / yet
4. the contestants / get ready / still
5. the guest celebrity / not arrive / yet

Speaking

12 **Work in groups. Why are these people famous? Do you think all celebrities are talented?**

Prince William — Stella McCartney
Paris Hilton — Ashton Kutcher

Study skills

Identifying the main idea in a text

1. Read the headline or title of the text. It usually summarises the most important information.
2. Look for information in the text that supports the headline. This is usually in the first or second sentence.
3. Read the whole text.

1C Exchanging opinions

Reading and listening

1 **Look at the photo. What do you think is happening?**

2 1.5 **Read and listen to the dialogue. Who likes Wayne Hill? Who doesn't like him?**

3 **Read the dialogue again. Find the adjectives that are used to describe Wayne Hill. Are they positive or negative?**

Dan: Wow, look at all these people! Wayne Hill's really popular!

Joe: Of course he is. I think he's brilliant. He's the most talented celebrity in England!

Holly: I don't think so, actually.

Joe: Why not?

Holly: Because he doesn't dance very well. He's quite funny and entertaining, but he's clumsy when he dances.

Fay: That's true. He seems a bit arrogant to me.

Dan: Do you think so?

Fay: Yes, I do.

Joe: Well, I think that's because he's really motivated. He always tries to win.

Fay: I know, but … oh, it's hard to explain.

Holly: I know what you mean. He sometimes seems unfriendly.

Dan: Actually, I've read his autobiography. Joe lent it to me. He's had a fascinating life, in my opinion.

Fay: Why do you say that?

Dan: Oh, because he's done so many different things and he's still only 25.

Holly: Look, the queue is moving forwards! We're nearly there.

Joe: Oh, I can't wait to meet him! It's so exciting!

Holly: Calm down, Joe!

Five minutes later

Joe: Wow! Look, he's written, 'To Joe, go for it! Wayne Hill.'

Holly: Yeah … and I've changed my mind, Joe. Wayne Hill isn't unfriendly at all. I think he's really nice!

4 **Find the *Useful expressions* in the dialogue. Match the functions (1–3) with the headings (a–c).**

1 giving an opinion
2 giving reasons for your opinion
3 reacting to an opinion

USEFUL EXPRESSIONS

a I think he's brilliant.
He seems a bit arrogant to me.
... in my opinion. / In my opinion, ...
b I don't think so. I know what you mean.
That's true. Why do you say that?
Do you think so?
c Because he doesn't dance very well.
That's because he's really motivated.

5 1.6 **Listen and repeat the *Useful expressions*. Focus on your intonation.**

6 1.7 **Listen to each statement and choose the best response (a–c).**

1 a In my opinion, he dances very well.
b Because it's entertaining.
c I know what you mean.

2 a Do you think so?
b I think he's popular.
c Yes, I do.

3 a That's true.
b I think it's brilliant.
c Because she makes me laugh.

Speaking

7 **Work in pairs. Put the sentences in order. Then practise the dialogue.**

a I think *TV Star* magazine is fascinating!
b Oh, because it's full of celebrity gossip.
c That's true. But it seems a bit repetitive to me.
d Well, I don't think so.
e Why do you say that?

8 **Work in pairs. Read the statements below and think about your opinions. Then work in groups and discuss each statement. Use the *Useful expressions* to help you.**

1 Reality TV is rubbish!
2 U2 – the best band of all time!
3 Too much TV makes people stupid.
4 Everybody wants to be famous these days.

Pronunciation: *-ght* and *-ghed*

9 1.8 **Listen and repeat the past participles. Which two are different to the others?**

bought brought caught coughed
fought laughed taught thought

10 **Write sentences with four of the past participles. Give them to your partner to read aloud. Who has the best pronunciation?**

Writing: a review

1 **Read Holly's review of a TV show. Write the number of the paragraph next to the information.**

good points bad points
a conclusion details and format

2 **Find five expressions Holly uses to introduce an opinion.**

3 **Holly uses *because* and *because of* to explain her opinion. Find these expressions in the review. Then complete the sentences with *because* or *because of*.**

1 Talent shows are exciting .... they are emotional.
2 *Avatar* was a success .... its special effects.
3 This show works .... the celebrity guests.
4 I love *Friends* .... it's always funny.

See Grammar Explorer: Page 118

1 *Young Tycoon* is a new reality TV show. Students aged 13–21 compete to make the most money. They have to try out a different business idea every week. There are three judges who set the tasks.

2 On the one hand, it's an entertaining show. I think this is because of the contestants. They're really ambitious and motivated. They're fascinating to watch because they get totally involved with the tasks.

3 On the other hand, the business ideas seem dull to me. In my opinion, washing cars (the idea in Episode 1) is not especially exciting television! In my view, reality TV shows work best when viewers can vote for the contestants, and *Young Tycoon* isn't interactive like that.

4 In conclusion, I'd watch *Young Tycoon* once a week, but not every night.

4 **Write a review of a TV show you have seen. Use Holly's review to help you.**

1D New Zealand on film

Reading

1 **Look at the photos and the text quickly. What's the main subject of the article?**

a a film about New Zealand wildlife
b New Zealand actors and directors
c the New Zealand film industry

2 **Work in pairs. Student A, read sections 1 and 2. Student B, read sections 3 and 4. Then close your books and tell your partner three things you remember.**

3 **Read your partner's sections and check the information they have given you.**

4 **Look at the example. Rewrite the pairs of sentences as one sentence.**

e.g. Wellington is not only the capital of New Zealand but also the capital of the country's film industry.

1 Weta is the name of a studio. It is also an insect.
2 Fiordland is the location of the Dead Marshes. It's the location of Rivendell too.
3 Some film locations are remote. They are also dangerous.
4 Russell Crowe is talented. He is famous too.

Culture

1 Welcome to 'Wellywood'!

Wellington + Hollywood = Wellywood.
Wellington is not only the capital of New Zealand but also the capital of the country's hugely successful film industry. Just some of the films made here are: *King Kong*, *The Chronicles of Narnia*, *Wolverine*, *Avatar* and perhaps the most famous of all, the *Lord of the Rings* trilogy. That's why, as well as *Wellywood*, the city is often nicknamed *Middle-earth*. Wellington's film production studios include the special effects experts, Weta Digital.

2 Location, location!

New Zealand has stunning scenery. It's perfect for the fantasy world of many films. Do you remember Aslan's camp in *The Chronicles of Narnia*? It's actually Elephant Rocks on South Island. Now thousands of film fans from all over the world are visiting New Zealand to see the places in their favourite films. One of the most popular and thrilling trips is a tour of Fiordland to see the 'real' Dead Marshes, Rivendell and Fanghorn Forest.

3 Essential New Zealand film jargon

Weta is not just the name of a studio, the weta is actually a native New Zealand insect. Its Maori name means 'god of ugly things'. The giant weta is about 90mm long and weighs 70 grams.
Bigature = big + miniature. This is the name for very large models that are still much smaller than the real thing. Do you remember the city of Minas Tirith in *Lord of the Rings*? That's a 'bigature'.
Massive software was invented to generate thousands of images for amazing crowd scenes like the battles in *Lord of the Rings*. You can see its effects in films like *Happy Feet*, *Wall-E* and *I, Robot* too.

4 Did you know?

- The giant-sized attacking insects in *King Kong* are computer-generated Weta.
- King Kong's roar is a lion's roar, played backwards at half speed.
- Some film locations are so remote that actors and crew can only get there by helicopter and they have to take survival kits.
- *Gladiator* star Russell Crowe was born in New Zealand.

Listening

5 **Have you seen these films? What can you remember about the places in them? Tell your partner.**

Braveheart	The Bourne Ultimatum
Harry Potter	The Da Vinci Code

6 1.9 **Listen to Casey, who is is on a film tour of the UK. Which places does he mention?**

a capital city	a lake
a cathedral	a castle
a valley	a church
a station	a casino

7 1.9 **Listen again and match the places with the films.**

8 **Do you know any film locations in your country? Tell your partner.**

Social science and English

Media studies

1 **Read the quotation. What do you think it means?**

'If you don't read the newspaper, you are uninformed; if you do read the newspaper, you are misinformed.'

Mark Twain, 1835–1910.

2 **Work in pairs. Read the text and answer the questions marked 'Q'**

Newspapers and magazines organise different kinds of information into different sections. Some of this information is factual, for example national news or sports reports. These sections tell us what's happening in the world. Other sections give opinions – they tell us what people think about what's happening, for example film and music reviews or celebrity features.

Q *Choose a newspaper or magazine you have read. How many different sections are there? Do you know if they are factual or opinion? How do you know?*

Both factual reports and opinion articles can be subjective. News stories are not always reported in the same way. Journalists can report events from different points of view. Look at these headlines from two reports of the same Formula 1 race in Australia.

Another disappointing race for Hamilton

Jensen Button is the greatest!

One headline emphasises a negative aspect of the race; the other is positive. Both headlines are from British media, but look at this third headline from an Australian paper. The story is about the location, not the drivers.

Spectacular racing at Melbourne once again!

Q *Which headline is negative? Who do you think won the race? Why do you think the Australian headline refers to the location?*

3 **When you read or listen to the news, think about these questions.**

- Is this a factual story, an opinion or the journalist's point of view?
- What aspect of the story is emphasised?
- Can different people interpret this story in different ways?
- What do other media say about the same story?

Project

Work in pairs. Choose an international story that is in the news at the moment. Then choose two different kinds of media, for example the Internet and a newspaper. Write the story in the style of each media.

TRUE STORY

Music explorer

Charlie Gillett was an explorer and a pioneer who travelled the world in search of what mattered to him most. But Charlie wasn't looking for hidden treasure or lost tribes; Charlie was motivated by music. His explorations led him to discover hugely talented musicians from around the world. He then introduced these new sounds to thousands of other people through his entertaining and informative radio shows.

In 1970 Charlie wrote a book about the history of rock and roll. Then it was while working as a music journalist that Charlie began his career as a radio broadcaster. What made him so fascinating to listen to was his knowledge of the music and his genuine enthusiasm for new bands and performers. He turned down the chance to present a popular TV programme because, as he said, he would have found it difficult to introduce bands who he didn't find exciting.

It was on the radio that Charlie felt most comfortable and he eventually turned his attention to playing music from outside of Britain and the US. Charlie was partly responsible for the phrase *world music*, which is how we now refer to this type of music. Later, he often travelled abroad, keen to meet local musicians and to bring home recordings of music which he could play to his growing audience in Britain.

Each year from 2000 to 2009, Charlie helped create a series of CDs highlighting the best talents of world music. By the time of his death in 2010, Charlie had become one of the most respected figures in broadcasting. Thanks to his hard work, many of his discoveries became hugely successful performing artists.

1 Read the information and choose the correct endings (a or b) for the sentences.

1. Charlie explored different countries to look for
   - **a** hidden treasure and lost tribes.
   - **b** talented musicians.
2. Audiences liked Charlie because he
   - **a** knew a lot about the music he presented.
   - **b** played songs that people knew well.
3. Charlie was
   - **a** keen to break into television broadcasting.
   - **b** happiest presenting radio programmes.
4. Later in his career, Charlie
   - **a** became more interested in world music.
   - **b** focused on music from Britain and the US.
5. Many performers benefited from Charlie's
   - **a** expert knowledge of music.
   - **b** enthusiasm for different sounds.
6. Charlie helped produce CDs of
   - **a** music he had made himself.
   - **b** important world music performers.

2 Match these words to their meanings.

1	pioneer (1)	**a**	important
2	tribes (1)	**b**	refused
3	influential (2)	**c**	appreciated
4	turned down (2)	**d**	the first person to do something
5	respected (3)	**e**	groups of people

3 Talk about one or more of the following questions with a partner.

- Can you name any popular performers from outside Britain and the US?
- How easy is it to discover new music from different countries?
- Which performers from your country do you think deserve a wider audience? Why?

2 The mind

> Grammar

Learn about the present perfect continuous, relative clauses, and question tags.

> Vocabulary

Learn words connected with the mind, and adjectives to describe personality.

Work with abstract nouns, and verb + *-ing*.

> Skills

Read about the cleverest animals known to science, hypnosis, and Irish traditions.

Listen to a podcast about phobias, and a survey about beliefs.

Write a description of people.

> Communicate

Check information.

1 Work in pairs. What do you think the orangutan is thinking about?

2 Complete the questions with words from the vocabulary box. How many questions can you make?

Can animals ... ? Have you got a good ... ?
When do you feel ... ?

afraid	happy	remember
angry	imagination	sad
creative	imagine	think
feel	intelligent	understand
forget	memory	

3 2.1 Listen to part of a documentary. Which of your questions do you hear?

4 Work in groups. Choose three of your questions from Exercise 2 and discuss your answers.

2A Animal minds

MEET THE cleverest animals KNOWN TO SCIENCE ...

Edward

Kanzi

Betsy

There are some skills which are key signs of intelligence in humans. They include memory, creativity and communication. Recently, scientists have been investigating these skills in animals too. They've found out some surprising things!

1 ....

Biologist Keith Kendrick has been testing the memory of sheep like Edward for several years. He's proved that sheep can remember faces for about two years. They recognise both other sheep and humans, and they prefer faces that show happiness to anger or fear!

2 ....

In the wild, orangutans make leaves into rain hats, pillows and even gloves. Orangutans are expert tool users. An orangutan called Fu Manchu has escaped from a zoo three times, using a piece of wire to unlock his cage. Scientists have been studying how animals use tools since 1960, when Jane Goodall first reported it. They've discovered that in addition to primates, elephants, many birds and even octopuses use tools.

3 ....

Kanzi is a bonobo. Bonobos are a type of chimpanzee which only live in the Congo, but Kanzi has always lived in captivity. He's been 'talking' to humans since he was a baby. He's learned to use more than 360 keyboard symbols and he understands thousands of spoken words. He's been playing the piano for us this morning. He's pretty good at it – he's even played with Paul McCartney! And finally, meet Betsy, who has been busy today too. She's been running around, collecting objects for researchers. Betsy is so clever that she understands pictures as well as spoken words. So, when you show her a photo of a ball, she brings you a ball. Do you think she'll recognise herself in this photo?

Reading and listening

1 **Look at the photos. Which of the three animals do you think is the most intelligent? Explain your opinion to your partner.**

2 **Choose the correct verb. Then decide if you think the sentences are true or false.**

1. Sheep can **imagine** / **remember** faces.
2. Primates can **think** / **forget** about answers to problems.
3. Some dogs **feel** / **understand** pictures of objects.

3 **Read the text quickly. Check your answers to Exercise 2.**

4 2.2 **Read and listen to the text. Complete the gaps (1–3) with the headings. There is one extra heading.**

Communication Creativity
Fear Memory

Working with words: abstract nouns

5 **Look at the examples. Find five more abstract nouns in the text.**

intelligence
memory

See Working with words: Page 101

Grammar: present perfect continuous

6 **Look at the examples. Which verbs do we use to make the present perfect continuous?**

e.g. Scientists have been investigating these skills in animals.
Keith Kendrick has been testing the memory of sheep like Edward for several years.

7 **Complete the table with the words in the box.**

'ye been | has | hasn't been | have | haven't been

Affirmative
He's been testing his memory. We (**1**) .... studying sheep.
Negative
She (**2**) .... practising the piano. They (**3**) .... paying attention.
Questions
(**4**) .... you been running? (**5**) .... he been playing the piano?

We use the present perfect continuous to talk about recent or unfinished activities. We use the present perfect simple to talk about the results of recent activities.

See Grammar Explorer: Page 118

8 **Match the activities (1–4) with the results (a–d).**

1 Keith Kendrick has been testing the memory of sheep.
2 Scientists have been investigating intelligence in animals.
3 Researchers have been showing Betsy photos.
4 I've been thinking about the problem.

a I've decided to ask my teacher.
b He's proved that they can remember faces.
c She's brought them lots of objects.
d They've found out some surprising things!

9 **Complete the sentences with the present perfect continuous form of the verbs in the box.**

look for | not practise | think about | wait for | watch

1 Look at the time! We .... you since four o'clock.
2 There it is! My mum .... that book for days!
3 'You're brilliant at this!' 'Really? I ....'
4 I'm exhausted! I .... this maths problem for hours.
5 Switch off that TV. You .... it all day!

Speaking

10 **Work in pairs. Ask and answer questions about the pictures. Use the verbs in the box.**

A: *What has the boy been doing?*
B: *I think he's been eating chocolate.*

dig | drink | eat | hide | play | read | run | study

Verbs like *be, know, believe, like*, etc. do not usually have a continuous form.

11 **Complete the questions using the present perfect continuous or simple. Then work in pairs. Ask and answer the questions. Use *for* or *since* in your answers.**

1 How long .... (**learn**) English?
2 How long .... (**know**) your best friend?
3 How long .... (**be**) in this class?
4 How long .... (**do**) this exercise?
5 How long .... (**have**) your school bag?

Fast finishers

Write an A–Z of animals. How many letters can you use?

2B Mind control

HYPNOSIS – controlling the mind

It's Friday evening and the Tennant family are at home in front of the TV. The programme is fascinating – they haven't moved for an hour. In fact, they seem to be stuck to the sofa, unable to move! They've been watching Derren Brown. He's the hypnotist whose weekly TV show attracts millions of viewers. In the programme, which is live, Brown has tried to hypnotise the audience so that they can't stand up. It's a huge experiment in mind control.

Hypnotising people through the TV is very unusual, although we've probably all seen hypnosis acts on TV. The hypnotist uses methods like swinging a watch, counting backwards or repeating phrases to make people 'sleep'. Then the hypnotist makes the people, who are usually volunteers, do silly things. People who are shy become sociable. Introverts become extroverts. People imagine they are animals, and so on. These changes in people's behaviour, which are funny and entertaining for the audience, are temporary. The volunteers don't become creative or clever if they weren't like that before. And after the show, they can't remember what they've been doing.

However, lots of people believe that hypnosis can change behaviour and habits which cause them problems. Many people have stopped smoking after hypnosis or have cured phobias, such as the fear of flying or snakes. One man, whose life was changed by hypnosis, even gave up his job and trained as a hypnotist so that he could help other people!

But let's go back to the Tennant family. At the end of Brown's programme, he sends a secret message that 'frees' the viewers who are stuck (or believe they're stuck!) and life in the Tennant home can go back to normal!

Speaking

1 Look at the photos.
Do you think these things are frightening?

2 Work in pairs. What are you afraid of? How do you react when you are afraid? Tell your partner.

Listening

3 2.3 **Listen to a podcast about phobias. Tick the photos you hear about.**

4 2.3 STUDY SKILLS **Listen again and make notes on the phobias.**

Phobia = fear of things that ....
Common phobias: fear of .... , ... , ...
Physical signs: sweating and ....
Unusual phobias: .... , ...

Reading and listening

5 **Look at the photos in Exercise 1 again. Then read the text quickly. Are any of the things mentioned in the text?**

6 2.4 **Read and listen to the text. Answer the questions.**

1. What does Derren Brown do in his TV show?
2. Why do people find hypnosis acts entertaining?
3. How can hypnosis help people?

7 **STUDY SKILLS** **Read the text and complete the notes. Compare with your partner.**

Derren Brown: a ....
Derren Brown's TV show: ....
Methods of hypnosis: .... , ... , ...
Hypnosis can cure: .... , ... , ...

Working with words: verb + *-ing*

8 **Look at the examples. Find five more activities with this form in the text.**

control → controlling
smoke → smoking

See Working with words: Page 101

Grammar: relative clauses

9 **Look at the examples. Find the relative clause in each sentence. Which relative clause can be omitted from the sentence because it gives extra information?**

1. People who are shy become sociable.
2. The people, who are usually volunteers, do silly things.

See Grammar Explorer: Page 119

10 **Find six more sentences with relative clauses in the text. Find the relative clauses which give extra information.**

We use the relative pronouns *who, which,* and *whose*, and the relative adverbs *when* and *where* in both types of sentence. We only use *that* in sentences which don't give extra information.

11 **Look at the example. Then rewrite each pair of sentences, putting the second sentence inside the first. Use the relative pronoun or adverb. Be careful with the position of the commas.**

The programme is very popular. It lasts one hour. (which)

e.g. The programme, which lasts one hour, is very popular.

1. Derren Brown is a hypnotist. He's from London. (who)
2. Brown's show is fascinating. It's on TV. (which)
3. Friday night is the best night of the week. We watch Brown's show. (when)
4. This hypnotist is American. His act is great. (whose)
5. Los Angeles is a centre for hypnosis therapies. This hypnotist lives in Los Angeles. (where)

12 **Work in pairs. Do you agree with the definition? Write more definitions for the words in the box.**

People who are creative have a good imagination and can make original things.

clever	creative	extrovert	funny
imaginative	introvert	logical	moody
organised	practical	shy	sociable

Speaking

13 **Work in groups. Discuss the questions.**

1. Do you believe hypnosis works?
2. Have you ever seen a hypnotist?
3. Would you like to be hypnotised?

Study skills

Making notes

1. Listen or read for the main points.
2. Note down key words and additional information.
3. Use abbreviations, such as: =, &, etc.

2C Checking information

Reading and listening

1 2.5 **Dan, Fay and Joe are at Holly's house. Read and listen to the dialogue. What two things do they need for their presentation?**

2 **Read the dialogue again. Choose the correct option.**

1 They **have** / **haven't** got two weeks to prepare.
2 Joe **has** / **hasn't** brought the script.
3 Dan **wants** / **doesn't want** to do the introduction.

3 **Choose the correct option. Then find two more questions with this form. Match each question with one of the options.**

Dan asks 'Isn't the presentation on the 18th?' because **he's surprised** / **he expects the listener to agree**.

4 **We also use tags to check information. Look at the example and find four similar questions in the dialogue.**

He's lovely, isn't he?

See Grammar Explorer: Page 120

5 2.6 **Listen and repeat the *Useful expressions*. Focus on your intonation.**

USEFUL EXPRESSIONS

He's lovely, isn't he?
We've still got two weeks, haven't we?
You haven't forgotten it again, have you?
You're joking, aren't you?
You don't mind, do you?

Holly: Sorry I'm late. Have you been waiting long?
Fay: That's OK. We've been playing with your dog. He's really smart!
Holly: I know. He's lovely, isn't he?
Fay: Yes, he is. OK, shall we start? We haven't got much time.
Dan: We've still got two weeks, haven't we?
Fay: No, we haven't.
Dan: Isn't the presentation on the 18th?
Fay: No, it's on the eighth. And today's the second! Joe, have you brought the script?
Joe: Oh … erm …
Fay: Oh, Joe, you haven't forgotten it again, have you?
Joe: Sorry, I've got a really bad memory.
Holly: It's OK, I've got a copy on my memory stick. And I've got the slideshow on there too. Here you are.
Joe: Oh, Holly, you're very organised, as usual!
Holly: Well, my mum reminded me! Have you been practising the introduction, Dan?
Dan: Oh dear, not really, no.
Holly: Don't you want to do it?
Dan: I'm not sure. I think I've got a public speaking phobia!
Joe: You're joking, aren't you? You're not usually shy!
Dan: Can't I do the slideshow instead? You don't mind, do you?
Joe: Hey, no problem! I'll do the introduction.

6 2.7 **Read and complete Holly's questions on the day of the presentation. Choose the correct option (a–b). Then listen and check your answers.**

1 You've got your memory stick, ... ?
 a have you **b** haven't you
2 The slide show is ready, ... ?
 a is it **b** isn't it
3 You know what to say, ... ?
 a do you **b** don't you
4 Dan's here, ... ?
 a is he **b** isn't he
5 You're not nervous, ... ?
 a are you **b** aren't you

Pronunciation: question tag intonation

7 2.7 **Listen again to the questions from Exercise 6. Which question tag does not have falling intonation? Repeat the questions.**

1 You've got your memory stick, haven't you?

We use a falling intonation when we expect the person to agree.

Speaking

8 **Look at the example. Complete the questions. Then ask and answer the questions with your partner. Give true answers.**

e.g. It's Sunday today, isn't it?

A: *It's Sunday today, isn't it?*
B: *No, it isn't.*

1 It isn't cold today, ... ?
2 You're not fifteen, ... ?
3 We haven't got maths today, ... ?
4 You're good at English, ... ?
5 You don't speak Italian, ... ?

9 **How well do you know your partner? Choose one of the options and complete each question. Then ask and answer the questions.**

1 You **like** / **don't like** football, ... you?
2 You**'ve got** / **haven't got** relatives in the USA, ... you?
3 You **can** / **can't** swim 500 metres, ... you?
4 You**'re** / **aren't** scared of snakes, ... you?
5 You**'ve been** / **haven't been** to London, ... you?

Writing: a description of people

1 **Read Dan's description of his family. Find the adjectives he uses to describe them.**

2 **Read the extra information. Match the relative clauses (a–e) with the places in the text (1–5).**

a when we are all at home
b where she spends all her time
c which we aren't allowed to see
d who lives with us
e whose name is Anna

3 **Complete the sentences with the correct relative pronoun.**

1 My mum, ... is scared of cats, wants to get a dog.
2 My best friend, ... desk is next to mine, is called Ali.
3 On Fridays, ... we all meet, we go to the cinema.
4 My room, ... I do my homework, is quite messy.
5 My friend's jokes, ... I've heard before, aren't funny.

4 **Choose a group of people you know well. Make notes about each person. Then write a short text describing the people.**

Name	Personality	Example	Extra information
my grandma	really bossy	likes giving orders	lives with us

My family

Everybody in my family has a strong personality, but we all get on well together. My grandma (1) , ... , is really bossy. She likes giving us all orders.

My parents are quite similar to each other. They're both practical and good at fixing things. And they both think they are always right!

My sister (2) , ... , can be a bit moody. Communication is not her strong point! She likes painting and her bedroom (3) , ... , is full of her work. She's been working on her latest picture (4) , ... , for about a week. My brother loves jokes and funny stories. In the evenings (5) , ... , he talks all the time. He likes telling jokes that he gets off the Internet. He's a lot more entertaining than the TV!

All in all, we're a happy family – most of the time!

2D Irish traditions

Reading

1 Do you know what the words in the box mean? Find them in the text. Then match them with the definitions (a–e). There is one extra definition.

a fairy	folklore	a lament	nocturnal

a a type of sad song
b appearing at night
c you can't see it
d old stories and beliefs
e a magical creature

2 2.8 **Read and find the following information.**

1 three things which are unlucky
2 three things that are lucky
3 three things about Irish fairies
4 four types of Irish fairies

Culture

Ireland is a country of traditions and folklore. Many of these are about luck and superstition.

There are lots of Irish superstitions to encourage good luck and avoid bad luck. Even today, many people are still quite superstitious in everyday life. For example, they avoid black cats, opening an umbrella indoors or putting shoes on a table. If you need good luck, try hanging a horseshoe on your front door or carrying a rabbit's foot. The luckiest thing of all is a four-leaf shamrock – but if you find one, don't tell anyone or your luck will disappear.

Many people belive that fairies still live all over Ireland. The worst thing you can do is to offend one of them because they can bring you bad luck. However, as they are invisible to humans most of the time, you have to be very careful! One of the best-known fairies is the leprechaun. He's about a metre tall and usually wears green. Leprechauns think humans are foolish and greedy, and they love tricking us. According to tradition, leprechauns carry two coins. One is gold, the other silver. When a leprechaun buys something with the silver coin, it always returns to him. If he gives you the gold coin, it turns to ashes when he leaves. Female fairies include the banshee and the beautiful merrow. The merrow, who lives in the sea, can be dangerous for sailors and fishermen. The banshee sings a lament when a person dies. Both can appear in different forms, depending on which part of Ireland they are in. This is also true of the ugly, scary pooka. These are evil nocturnal fairies who enjoy frightening farm animals and farmers.

Irish people are also famous for giving guests a fantastic welcome, so perhaps the luckiest people in Ireland are the people who go there to visit.

3 **Read the statements (1–3) and match each one with a type of fairy mentioned in the text.**

1 They are always male, never female.
2 Their song can be beautiful or like an animal noise.
3 They stop hens from laying eggs.

4 **Look at the words in red in the text. What or who do they refer to?**

5 **Work in pairs. Are there any similar beliefs and legends in your country? Tell your partner.**

Listening

6 **Work in pairs. Do you believe in these things? Or are you not sure? Explain your answers.**

1 ghosts and haunted houses
2 witches
3 UFOs
4 astrology
5 predicting the future
6 spiritual healing

7 2.9 **A survey asked American people about the things in Exercise 6. Listen and write the numbers (per cent) of people who believe in each thing.**

1 ....
2 ....
3 ....
4 ....
5 ....
6 ....

8 2.9 **Listen again. Is the number of people who aren't sure about each thing bigger or smaller?**

1 ....
2 ....
3 ....
4 ....
5 ....
6 ....

Project

Work in groups. Research a story on one of the topics in Exercise 6. Prepare a presentation for the class.

Biology and English

Animals and people

1 **Look at the mind map. What information do you think goes in the gaps?**

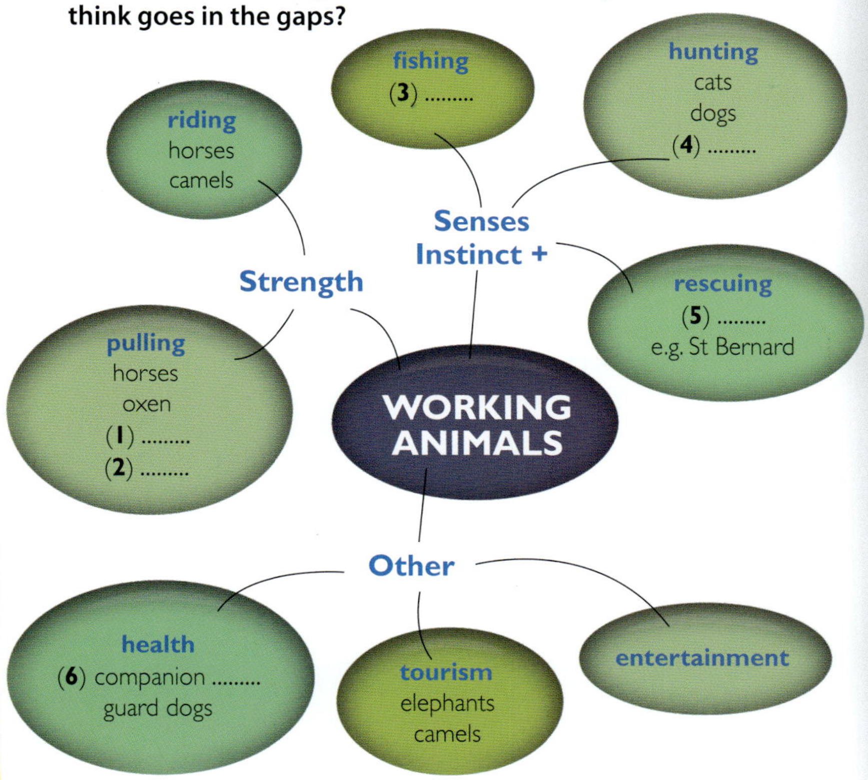

2 **Read the text and complete the mind map.**

Throughout history, humans have had close associations with certain animals. The ancient Egyptians even believed that cats were gods. People have used animals to help them with work, using their strength and their highly developed senses for different purposes. Horses and oxen can pull heavy farm machinery, for example, while huskies and reindeer can pull sleds across snowy ground.

Some animals have instincts that humans can exploit for hunting other animals and food. In China birds called cormorants catch fish for their human owners, and pigs are very good at finding truffles (a special kind of mushroom) in the ground. Dogs have a fantastic sense of smell and they are better than machines at finding people who are trapped under avalanches or by earthquakes. They are just as good at sniffing out drugs and finding criminals too.

Sometimes animals can work for us as well as with us. Doctors say that our stress levels go down and that we become happier and healthier when we have a pet for company. Companion dogs are dogs which visit elderly people, patients in hospital and even people in prison. We also enjoy animals as entertainment, as the success of movies like *Free Willy* and *Babe* show!

3 **Work in pairs. Add at least three more animals to the mind map in Exercise 1.**

Consolidation Units 1 and 2

Reading

Identifying the main ideas of sections of a text

- Read the whole text quickly before you look at the headings and identify the main idea in each section.
- If the headings are questions, predict the kind of information that answers the question. Then look for this information in the text.
- **Important!** If there is an extra heading, make sure it doesn't match any of the sections.

1 Find the words that help you decide on the main idea of these sections of a text.

1 There are both 'good' dreams and 'bad' dreams (nightmares). Some kinds of dream are quite common. Typical dreams can be about flying, water or trees. Some are in colour and others are in black and white.

2 There are different interpretations of dreams. A bad dream can mean something good – that you will be lucky or happy. Some people don't believe that dreams have meanings.

2 Match the correct heading (a–c) with each section (1–2) in Exercise 1. There is one extra heading.

a my dreams
b the meaning of dreams
c types of dream

3 Read part of a text about 'memory' and match the correct heading (a–c) with each section (1–2).

1 Yes. Eating 'brain food' which has lots of vitamins is one way. Protein is also good for your memory. But the best way is to use your brain more.

2 This is our ability to remember things that happened very recently, for example a few minutes ago. The brain stores this new information in a special way.

a Why have I got a bad memory?
b Can I improve my memory?
c What is short-term memory?

Listening

Identifying detailed information

- Read the task and the options before listening.
- For text options, think about the pronunciation of each option.
- For picture options, think about what distinguishes each option.
- **Important!** Don't try to understand everything. Listen only for the answers to the questions.

1 Look at the pictures below and write as many words as you can for each one.

2 Choose the words in your list that show the differences between the pictures. Add more words which show the differences to your list.

3 2.10 **Listen to the conversation. Which animal are they talking about?**

A

B

C

Adverbs of frequency

Adverbs of frequency go before the main verb, except when the verb is *be*.

She always wears black.
She's never worn brown.
Her clothes are never colourful.

1 Mark the correct position of the adverbs.

1. I don't do my homework with my friends. (usually)
2. I'm shy when I meet new people. (sometimes)
3. We watch TV in the morning. (never)
4. My dad is funny at parties. (always)

both, all

All and *both* go before the main verb, except when the verb is *be*. They can also go before the subject of the verb.

2 Mark the two possible positions of *all* and *both*.

1. My parents are vegetarians. (both)
2. My brother and I can play the piano. (both)
3. My friends like sport. (all)
4. This summer my cousins and I are going camping. (all)

Adverbs of place and time

Adverbs of time usually go after adverbs of place.

I'm going to bed early.

3 Complete the sentences with the information in the box. Use two pieces of information in each sentence. How many sentences can you make?

before lunchtime	for ages	home
last summer	late	to school
to Scotland	to the cinema	

1. Did you go .... ?
2. I don't want to get ....
3. We haven't been ....
4. Please be ....

enough

Enough goes after adjectives and before nouns.

4 Mark the correct position of *enough*.

1. You aren't strong to lift that box.
2. My class is good to win the competition.
3. Are there people to play football?
4. We don't have time to prepare well.

Phrasal verbs

Some phrasal verbs have an object. We can put the object in two positions when it is a noun. The object pronoun only has one possible position.

She tried on the shoes.
She tried the shoes on.
She tried them on.

5 For each sentence, write two more sentences with the same meaning. Use a pronoun in one of the sentences.

1. I switched on the TV.
2. I found out the answers.
3. I picked the bags up.
4. I turned the computer off.

Questions

Be careful with word order in negative questions, indirect questions and questions with prepositions.

6 Look at the examples above and do the tasks.

1. Your friend doesn't want to come to a party. Ask him why not.
2. Rewrite the question: When does the film start?
   Do you know .... ?
3. Write a question for this answer.
   I'm thinking about my lunch.

Review Units 1 and 2

Vocabulary

1 Complete the sentences.

1 There are lots of c............ on satellite TV.
2 My mum's a j............ with the local paper.
3 I've read an a............ about hypnosis.
4 The h............ gives us the most important news.
5 *X Factor* got the biggest a............ last night.

1 mark per item: .../5 marks

2 Write the words.

1 He/She appears in films. a............
2 A practice performance. r............
3 He/She introduces TV shows. p............
4 One programme in a series. e............
5 He/She chooses the winner. j............

1 mark per item: .../5 marks

3 Complete the sentences with adjectives.

1 I don't like meeting people. I'm s............ .
2 He makes me laugh. He's f............ .
3 She makes beautiful things. She's c............ .
4 She writes amazing stories. She's i............ .
5 He always passes exams. He's c............ .

1 mark per item: .../5 marks

4 Complete the sentences with verbs.

1 Can fish f............ pain?
2 Do you u............ Chinese?
3 Can animals t............ about the future?
4 Can you r............ being a baby?
5 I can't i............ how big space is.

1 mark per item: .../5 marks

5 Complete the sentences.

1 Why are you staring .... me?
2 Come and talk .... us.
3 Are you a member of *Take That*'s fan .... ?
4 Don't lie. Tell me the ....
5 My dad's good at .... jokes.

1 mark per item: .../5 marks

Grammar

6 Complete the paragraph with the present simple or present continuous.

My dad (**1**) .... (**do**) a course of hypnosis. He (**2**) .... (**try**) to give up smoking because he (**3**) .... (**smoke**) too much. He (**4**) .... (**go**) to the hypnotist every day. Each session (**5**) .... (**take**) half an hour.

1 mark per item: .../5 marks

7 Complete the paragraph with the present simple, present continuous or present perfect.

A TV station (**1**) .... (**want**) to film our school and the head teacher (**2**) .... (**say**) 'yes'! The cameraman (**3**) .... (**film**) now. It's the first time we (**4**) .... (**be**) in front of a camera. We (**5**) .... (**not / do**) any lessons for days!

1 mark per item: .../5 marks

8 Mark the correct position of the words.

1 Have you finished that book? (**yet**)
2 No, I'm reading it. (**still**)
3 I haven't finished it. (**yet**)
4 The judges have started voting. (**already**)
5 I haven't seen Matt Damon's latest film. (**still**)

1 mark per item: .../5 marks

9 Write the present perfect continuous.

1 I'm tired. I .... all day. (**work**)
2 .... you .... my cake? (**eat**)
3 My dad .... well. (**not / feel**)
4 How long .... you .... ? (**wait**)
5 I .... TV very much recently. (**not / watch**)

1 mark per item: .../5 marks

10 Complete the sentences with *when, where, which, who* or *whose*.

1 The hypnotist, ... new show is great, is world-famous.
2 *Invictus*, ... stars Morgan Freeman, is about South Africa.
3 Matt Damon, ... is American, is in the film.
4 February, ... the Oscars are announced, is an exciting month.
5 Los Angeles, ... the ceremony is held, is in California.

1 mark per item: .../5 marks

Communicate

11 Match the statements and questions (1–5) with the responses (a–e).

1 What do you think of Dale Smith?
2 Do you like *Take That*?
3 Leona Lewis is amazing.
4 Why do you say that?
5 It's hard to explain what I think about hypnosis.

a Because they write good songs.
b He seems a bit arrogant to me.
c I know what you mean.
d Do you think so?
e Yes, I think they're great.

2 marks per item: .../10 marks

12 Complete the questions with question tags.

1 You can speak French, ... ?
2 It's not a holiday today, ... ?
3 We've got an exam tomorrow, ... ?
4 You like maths, ... ?
5 You're sixteen, ... ?

2 marks per item: .../10 marks

13 Do the words sound the same (S) as or different (D) from *bought*?

1 thought ....
2 laughed ....
3 caught ....
4 taught ....
5 coughed ....

2 marks per item: .../10 marks

14 Complete the sentences with *because* or *because of*.

1 I enjoy reality TV .... the people.
2 Kanzi was famous .... his skills.
3 I get this magazine .... I like animals.
4 Derren Brown is popular .... his TV shows.
5 I sometimes watch TV .... I'm bored.

2 marks per item: .../10 marks

15 Complete the review with these words.

a at for have on the their to which who

Magic Animals is a new TV series. It's (**1**) .... Channel Six on Wednesdays (**2**) .... 7 p.m. (**3**) .... first episode, (**4**) .... was on last night, was about dolphins. Apparently, dolphins can talk (**5**) .... each other in their own language. Scientists (**6**) .... been trying to understand this language (**7**) .... years. They explained (**8**) .... findings on this programme. In my view, this is (**9**) .... great series for anyone (**10**) .... likes animals.

1 mark per item: .../10 marks

Total: .../100

I can...

I can give my opinion and explain it.
I can react to someone else's opinion.
I can use question tags to check information..

Personality test

1 Read the information and answer the questions.

1. Why do people take a personality test?
2. How do you take a test?
3. What do you have to remember when taking a test?
4. Why is this type of testing called OCEAN?

There are many different reasons for using personality tests. These can include helping people with problems, finding out whether people are suitable for a job, or choosing the right kind of education for a child. Many researchers today use testing based on what they call the *Big Five*, also known as the *Five Factor Model* (FFM) or *OCEAN* (see box). By asking a series of questions, testers believe that they can identify what kind of person you are. For the person taking the test, however, it is important to understand that you must be honest when you answer the questions. There are no right or wrong answers, so do not choose an answer because you imagine it is the best thing to say. Depending on your answers, the tester can tell certain things about you, like whether you are more introverted or extroverted, or whether you are a logical and practical person.

The letters in the word OCEAN refer to the following characteristics:

Openness – describing people who are creative, adventurous and have a lot of imagination, and who like art and are open to new ideas and adventure

Conscientiousness – describing people who are organized and like to plan and achieve things

Extroversion – describing people who have a lot of energy and positive emotions, and enjoy the company of other people

Agreeableness – describing people who are friendly and work well with others

Neuroticism – describing people who easily feel sad or afraid, or have negative emotions such as anger

2 Now try a test for yourself. Answer *Yes* or *No* to each question. Remember to be honest with your answers.

1. You have been planning a day out. Is it likely to be somewhere you've never been before?
2. You have been working on a project all day. You're tired but you want to get it finished.
3. There is a new boy or girl at school. Are you probably the first person to speak to him or her?
4. Do you like working on exercises and projects with your classmates?
5. You have been waiting for five minutes and your friend hasn't arrived. Are you angry?

3 What do you think your answers say about you? Look at the list below and choose the correct word or phrase.

If you answered:

No to question **1**, you are probably **adventurous / not very adventurous**.

Yes to question **2**, you **are probably / are probably not** very conscientious.

No to question **3**, being friendly **is / is not** very important to you.

Yes to question **4**, you are probably quite **agreeable / difficult**.

No to question **5**, you probably **show / don't show** negative emotions.

Project

Write your own personality test and ask your friends to do it

- Choose questions similar to those above.
- You can ask about anything you like but try to keep the questions related to the characteristics in the OCEAN list.
- Ask your questions (you can do this by telephone or email if the person lives far away).
- Decide what you think the answers say about that person. You could say whether the answers suggest that the person is shy or sociable, organised, practical, imaginative, etc.
- Ask the other person if he or she agrees with you and discuss how well the test worked.

NATIONAL GEOGRAPHIC

In the past

3

> Grammar

Learn about the past perfect, and *used to*.

> Vocabulary

Learn words connected with time and archaeology, and for cooking. Work with verb + *to* + infinitive, and American English.

> Skills

Read about an amazing find, memories of the past, and American food.

Listen to recipe instructions and two meal-time conversations.

Write a recommendation.

> Communicate

Talk about quantity, time, distance, etc.

1 3.1 **Listen to the information about Stonehenge and make notes. Then compare your notes with your partner.**

Location? Age? Purpose?

2 **Put the words in the vocabulary box in order, from the shortest (1) to the longest (11) period of time.**

century	fortnight	minute	week
day	hour	month	year
decade	millennium	second	

3 **Find words in the vocabulary box for these periods of time.**

four weeks sixty seconds
a thousand years fourteen days

4 **Work in pairs. How many things can you remember that you did or that happened at these times?**

an hour ago in the last decade
last weekend during the Roman Empire
a year ago before the last Ice Age

3A Digging up the past

Ice Baby

A few years ago, a Nenet herder called Yuri Khudi was working with his reindeer in northern Siberia. In front of him, on the river bank, there was an unbelievable sight – a frozen baby mammoth. Mammoths lived about 40,000 years ago. They were hunted for food and their fossil remains tell us a lot about Stone Age life. It is very difficult to find artefacts, such as pottery or jewellery, from those times. Mammoth remains help us to understand how Stone Age people hunted.

Yuri had seen mammoth tusks and fragments of animals before, but he'd never seen a whole animal. He wasn't a palaeontologist so he wasn't sure what to do. He decided to ask a friend for advice. Together, they went to the local museum and spoke to the director. When they all got back to the river, Yuri was horrified – the baby mammoth had disappeared! Yuri got on his snowmobile and drove to the nearest town. Fortunately, it didn't take long to find the mammoth. Some local people had taken it from the river bank and sold it to a shop keeper! Yuri managed to get the mammoth back and it was taken to a museum. The museum officials wanted to thank Yuri, so they decided to call the baby mammoth Lyuba, in honour of Yuri's wife.

Palaeontologists from all over the world wanted to examine Lyuba. Their studies showed that the mammoth hadn't lived long – only one month. It had probably died after getting trapped in mud, and because of that it was so well preserved.

Reading and listening

1 **Work in pairs. Look at the words in the box. Find two words for professions and two words for places where these people can work.**

archaeologist	artefact	fossil	fragment
jewellery	palaeontologist	pottery	
remains	ruins	site	treasure

2 **Look at the story quickly. How many words from the vocabulary box can you find?**

3 3.2 **Read and listen to the story. What is it about? Choose the correct option (a–c).**

- **a** Ancient treasure found by an archaeologist.
- **b** An amazing find on an archaeological site.
- **c** An accidental discovery of ancient remains.

4 **Read the story again. Put each group of events in the order they actually took place.**

A
1 Yuri found a baby mammoth.
2 Yuri saw mammoth tusks.
3 Yuri talked to a museum director.

B
1 Yuri returned to the river bank.
2 Yuri went to a local shop.
3 Some people took the mammoth.

C
1 Palaentologists studied the mammoth.
2 The mammoth lived for one month.
3 The mammoth was taken to a museum.

Grammar: past perfect

5 Look at the example. Find five more past perfect verbs in the story.

Yuri had seen mammoth tusks before.

See Grammar Explorer: Page 120

6 Read the following sentence about an event in the story and choose the action that happened first.

When Yuri got back to the river, the mammoth had disappeared.

We use the past perfect to show that an event took place before other events we have mentioned.

7 Complete the sentences with the correct forms of the verbs: past simple or past perfect. The numbers give the order in which the events happened.

e.g. When the museum director (**arrive** – 2), the men (**leave** – 1).
When the museum director arrived, the men had left.

1. When Yuri (**talk** – 1) to the shop keeper, he (**give back** – 2) the mammoth.
2. When they (**find** – 2) the mammoth, it (**start** – 1) to thaw.
3. Yuri (**go** – 2) to the museum when he (**speak** – 1) to his friend.
4. Tests (**show** – 2) that the mammoth (**fall** – 1) into mud.
5. Palaeontologists (**can** – 2) learn a lot because the mammoth (**remain** – 1) frozen.

8 Write the correct form of the verbs: past simple or past perfect.

Modern archaeology (**1**) began (**begin**) in the 19th century. Before then, although people (**2**) .... (**dig up**) ruins, they (**3**) .... (**not use**) their discoveries in systematic studies. In the 19th century, archaeological sites in Italy, Greece and Egypt (**4**) .... (**become**) very popular. In Europe, lots of information (**5**) .... (**come**) from ancient rubbish tips where people (**6**) .... (**throw away**) their broken, unwanted objects. However, in Egypt archaeologists (**7**) .... (**hope**) to find valuable treasure. Often, tomb robbers (**8**) .... (**get**) there before them.

Working with words: verb + *to* + infinitive

9 Look at the example. Find two similar patterns in the text on page 30.

He decided to ask a friend for advice.

See Working with words: Page 102

Speaking

10 Work in pairs. Look at the pictures. Complete the sentences with the correct form of the verbs: past simple or past perfect.

At lunchtime I (**1**) .... (**open**) my lunchbox and I (**2**) .... (**realise**) that I (**3**) .... (**leave**) my lunch at home.

I (**4**) .... (**try**) to buy a sandwich, but I (**5**) .... (**not / can**) because I (**6**) .... (**not bring**) any money to school.

In the maths lesson I (**7**) .... (**look**) in my bag and I (**8**) .... (**see**) that I (**9**) .... (**forget**) my homework.

After school I (**10**) .... (**go**) to borrow a library book, but someone (**11**) .... (**already borrow**) it.

11 Ask and answer questions using the ideas in Exercise 10.

A: *What happened when you opened your lunchbox?*
B: *I realised I'd left my lunch at home.*

Fast finishers

There are two 'false friends' on this page and the opposite page. Can you find them?

3B Remembering the past

Speaking

1 **Work in pairs. What's your favourite meal? Have you always liked it – or have your tastes changed? Tell your partner.**

2 **Put the words in the box into two groups: *preparation* and *methods of cooking*. Use your dictionary. Which methods are used in your favourite meal?**

baking	boiling	chopping	frying
grilling	heating up	peeling	roasting
slicing			

Listening

3 **Look at the ingredients. What is the recipe for? Choose one of the options (a–c).**

a apple pie
b chocolate chip cookies
c chicken curry

250g butter

150g sugar

baking soda

300g flour

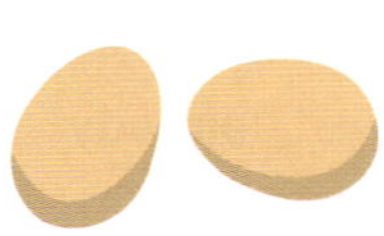
2 eggs

175g chocolate

4 3.3 **Listen and number the ingredients in the order you hear them.**

5 **STUDY SKILLS** 3.3 **Listen again and put the instructions in the correct order.**

a Add the chocolate.
b Add the flour and baking soda.
c Bake for 15 to 20 minutes.
d Heat the oven.
e Mix the sugar, butter and eggs.
f Put spoonfuls of the mixture on a baking tray.
g Put the tray into the oven.

Reading and listening

6 **Look at the photos (a–d) and read the texts (1–5) quickly. Which texts do the photos illustrate? There is one extra text.**

7 3.4 **Read and listen to people talking about memories of the past. Answer the questions.**

1 Which cooking methods are mentioned?
2 Find examples of food you can cook by each method.
3 Are the memories about regular activities or single events?

1

I used to love Sunday afternoons at home. Mum and I used to spend hours baking all sorts of cakes and biscuits. I think the idea was to feed the family for a week, but my brothers had big appetites. The cakes didn't use to last until Wednesday!

Jenny Watts, age 60

2

I'm American, so I grew up in the States. I remember the first TV dinners. My mom used to buy them at the store on a Saturday. She didn't use to cook them – they were already cooked. She just put them in the oven to heat up. Everything was in a separate section. I remember my favorite was roast beef and vegetables. Actually, they tasted awful!

Wayne Bridges, age 65

A

B

Grammar: *used to*

8 **Look at the text and complete the table.**

Used to
I (**1**) .... love Sunday afternoons at home.
Negative
She (**2**) .... cook them.
Questions
What (**3**) .... do before we had microwaves?

See Grammar Explorer: Page 121

3

We used to go camping every year with the school. It was brilliant! We used to cook our own food – we spent every evening grilling sausages, frying eggs and heating up tins of baked beans. Delicious!

Ronald Clark, age 16

4

Do you remember steak and kidney pie at school with boiled vegetables? And rice pudding? I always liked school dinners, but my best friend used to hate them. She used to swap her plate with a boy called Simon Evans. I think he's a famous chef now.

Denise Smith, age 21

5

Well, what did we use to do before we had microwaves? I really can't remember. I know it used to take ages to cook a meal in those days. Nowadays it only takes a few minutes. The latest models are so good you can even roast a chicken, I believe.

John Duffy, age 50

9 **Complete the text with the verbs in the box. Use the past simple or *used to*.**

ask be buy come go meet not answer put sell swim

When I was little, we (**1**) *used to go* swimming on Friday evenings. We (**2**) .... fish and chips afterwards. They (**3**) .... them wrapped in newspaper and (**4**) .... lots of salt on them. My sister only (**5**) .... with us once because she (**6**) .... scared of water. But she (**7**) .... us at the chip shop. The man in the shop always (**8**) .... us, 'How many lengths (**9**) .... you .... tonight?' But my sister (**10**) .... !

10 **Write five true or false sentences about your childhood. Then work in pairs and exchange your sentences. Find your partner's false sentences. Use ideas from the box and ideas of your own.**

e.g. *I didn't use to live in this town.*

comics food friends hobbies music pets school sports town TV

11 **Work in pairs. Ask and answer questions about your childhood.**

A: *Which comics did you use to read?*

B: *I used to read the* Beano.

Working with words: American English

12 **Look at the examples. How many American English words can you think of?**

cookie *n, US* a sweet biscuit, e.g. chocolate chip cookies

store *n, US* a shop, e.g. a shoe store

See Working with words: Page 102

Study skills

Listening for key words

1 Different kinds of texts can have different types of key words: verbs in instructions, past tenses in stories, adjectives in descriptions, etc.
2 Decide what kind of key words you need to listen for.
3 Focus on those words the first time you listen. Then listen for additional information.

3C Talking about quantity

Fay: Wow, Dan! That smells delicious!

Holly: Yeah, and it looks amazing too.

Fay: How long did it take you to make all this?

Dan: Oh, not long. About half an hour.

Holly: Really? How much did you make? There's enough food for ten people here!

Dan: No, there isn't!

Holly: So, Dan, when did you learn to make curry?

Dan: Oh, ages ago. My gran used to make it a lot.

Holly: I'm terrible at cooking. I once made a steak pie and it tasted absolutely disgusting. I'd put too much salt in it.

Fay: That doesn't sound too bad! I quite like salty food.

Holly: Well, the recipe said 10 grams and I put in 100 grams! Honestly, it was revolting!

Fay: What time are we eating, Dan?

Dan: At six, I hope. Joe phoned earlier. He's on his way, but he might be late. He's been to Stonehenge today.

Fay: How far is that? Isn't it quite a long way?

Holly: No, I think it's about 60 miles.

Fay: OK, then. Let's set the table. How many people are coming?

Dan: Just the four of us.

Holly: Fay, don't look now, but what are those packets in the bin?

Reading and listening

1 3.5 **Read and listen to the dialogue. Do you think Dan made the curry himself? Why? / Why not?**

2 **Read the dialogue again. Find the words that follow these phrases.**

1 That smells
2 it looks
3 it tasted
4 That doesn't sound

3 **Find the *Useful expressions* in the dialogue. How do you ask about these things?**

1 a period of time
2 a quantity of a countable thing
3 a quantity of an uncountable thing or of weight/ volume
4 a date
5 a distance
6 a time

USEFUL EXPRESSIONS

How long did it take you to make all this?
How much did you make?
When did you learn to make curry?
What time are we eating?
How far is that?
How many people are coming?

4 3.6 **Listen and repeat the *Useful expressions*. Focus on your intonation.**

Speaking

5 **Work in pairs. Complete the questions. Use the *Useful expressions* to help you. Then ask and answer the questions. Check your answers at the bottom of page 37.**

1 .... boil an egg?
   a 1 minute   b 10 minutes
   c 30 minutes

2 .... kilometres are in a mile?
   a 1.6 km   b 5 km   c 8.3 km

3 .... from London to New York?
   a 1,385km   b 5,585km
   c 8,573km

4 .... Stone Age man live?
   a 4,000 years ago   b 40,000 years ago
   c 400,000 years ago

5 .... a litre of water weigh?
   a 375 grams   b 1,000 grams
   c 1,200 grams

Pronunciation: words containing *ui*

6 3.7 **How do you pronounce these words? Compare with your partner. Then listen and repeat.**

biscuit building cruise fruit
guide juice liquid quick
quiet quite quiz ruins

Writing: a recommendation

1 **Read Fay's comments about the Jorvik Viking Centre. Which adjectives does she use?**

boring busy expensive
frightening good interesting
poor realistic

2 **Complete these sentences from the text.**

1 It was so busy ....
2 The street scenes were so realistic ....
3 We had such a good time ....

See Grammar Explorer: Page 121

3 **Rewrite the pairs of sentences using the words in brackets.**

1 The queue was long. We left. (**so**)
2 It was a realistic display. I was scared. (**such**)
3 It was a great place. I wanted to stay. (**such**)
4 It was a hot day. I needed a drink. (**such**)
5 I was hungry. I ate three sandwiches. (**so**)

4 **Choose a place you have visited – a tourist attraction, a town, a museum, etc. Make notes about its good and bad points, and what you did there. Then write a paragraph for a website to recommend (or not) the place.**

Jorvik Viking Centre

We visited the Jorvik Viking Centre last July. It was so busy that we had to queue for two hours to get in! But once we were inside, it was worth it. I went with my whole family (three generations) and we all enjoyed it. The street scenes were so realistic that the people looked alive! It's actually a bit frightening for very young children. We learned a lot about how the Vikings used to live over a thousand years ago. It was much more interesting than the stuff I'd done at school! The exhibitions are explained very well, so it didn't matter that we hadn't bought a guidebook. We had such a good time that my dad and I went back the next day. But I recommend that you avoid the busy tourist season – or be prepared to wait for a long time!

3D American food

Reading

1 **Have you ever eaten these foods? Are they used a lot in dishes in your country?**

cornbread pumpkin pie squash
mashed sweet potatoes roast turkey

2 3.8 **Read the text and answer the questions.**

1 When was the first 'thanksgiving' meal?
2 What did the first 'thanksgiving' meal celebrate?
3 How old is the tradition of Thanksgiving?

3 **Read the text again. How many foods can you find that are native to the Americas?**

4 **Find words in the text which match the definitions.**

1 a special meal with lots of different dishes
2 plants that provide food
3 the collection of food from plants
4 the opposite to a sweet taste

Culture

In every culture, food is a significant part of traditional celebrations. In the USA, the most important meal of the year is at Thanksgiving, which is always on the fourth Thursday in November. Thanksgiving celebrates a time in American history when the 'New World' and the 'Old World' began to mix. Almost 400 years ago, a group of English families arrived on the northeast coast of America – in an area which they called New England. During their first winter, they nearly ran out of the food they had brought with them. The local people, called the Wampanoag, showed them how to grow crops like corn and squash. The English had never seen these plants before as they were native to the New World. At the first harvest, the Wampanoag and the English (the Pilgrims) shared a feast that lasted for three days. This was the first 'thanksgiving' meal. However, the modern tradition only became popular at the end of the 19th century. These days, Thanksgiving is a day when families spend time together. It takes such a long time to make all the food that the whole family has to help. Then everyone sits down to enjoy the meal. Turkey, cornbread, sweet potatoes and pumpkin pie are always on the menu.

Many foods that we now think of as European originally came from the New World. Can you imagine Italian cooking without tomatoes? Or traditional English fish and chips without potatoes? Or life without chocolate? The Maya and Aztec peoples of Central and South America ate all of these things. They used to mix cacao with chilli to make a strong, bitter drink – that's a little different to a chocolate milkshake!

5 **Complete the sentences with the correct form of these verbs from the text.**

run out   last   spend   take

1 The festival usually .... for two days – from Saturday morning to Sunday night.
2 How do you like to .... your free time?
3 I can't finish the exam – I'm going to .... of time!
4 I hope you like your cake – it .... me hours to make it!

Listening

6 3.9 **Listen to two conversations. Where are the people? Write 1 or 2 next to the correct option (a–c).**

a at home
b in a restaurant
c in a school dining room

7 3.9 **Listen again and choose the correct answers (a–c).**

1 What are they eating?
   a packed lunches
   b a take-away
   c dessert
2 What dishes are mentioned?
   a cheesecake, fruit salad and tiramisu
   b cheesecake, ice cream and yogurt
   c chicken sandwiches, tuna salad and burgers
3 What's the occasion?
   a the last day of term
   b someone's birthday
   c passing an exam

Project

Choose a popular local or national celebration which has special food associated with it. Prepare a brochure for English visitors. Write a menu in English. Write a paragraph explaining the different dishes, their ingredients and how they are cooked.

KEY 1 b 2 a 3 b 4 b 5 b

Maths and English

The history of numbers

1 **Read the text. What is the difference between numbers and numerals?**

2 **Read the text again and work in pairs to answer the questions marked Q.**

This is the Ishango bone, which is about 20,000 years old. It was found in Africa, near where the River Nile begins. Scientists think that the marks on it are evidence that 20,000 years ago people used a counting system. Each mark equals 'one' – so two marks equal 'two', and so on. In Europe today, we use different symbols, or numerals, for different numbers. We use ten numerals, and we combine them to make other numbers.

0 1 2 3 4 5 6 7 8 9

These numerals came to Europe from the Arabic culture of North Africa, but they were originally invented in India in around 500 B.C. They are called Hindu-Arabic numerals. After their introduction to Europe around 1,000 A.D., it took several hundred years for the system to become commonly used. Until then, Europeans had used Roman numerals.

I V X L C D M

Q *How do you write the current year in Roman numerals?*

Both the Hindu-Arabic and the Roman systems are based on counting in groups of ten. The ancient Egyptians also had a system based on ten. Here are the hieroglyphics for 10, 100, 1,000 and 1,000,000.

Not all cultures counted in groups of ten. The Maya system used a combination of groups of four and five – together they made a group of twenty. These are the Maya symbols for 4, 5 and 6.

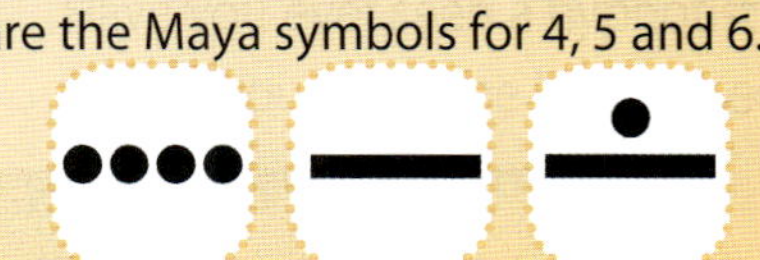

Q *Can you work out what these Maya numbers are?*

3 **Work in pairs. Why do you think different cultures counted in groups of four, five and ten?**

TRUE STORY

Mike Parker Pearson

Mike Parker Pearson is a professor of archaeology at Sheffield University, and his most recent explorations have been on the Stonehenge Riverside Project.

When Mike was four years old, some workers left a few stones in his garden. They contained lots of fossils, which sparked an interest in the young boy. By the time he was 14, Mike had been on his first archaeological dig, and a lifelong interest had begun. After he left Southampton University, Mike studied at Cambridge and took part in archaeological digs in Britain and many other countries.

Since 2003 Mike has directed projects at Stonehenge, where a major important discovery was the remains of Bluestonehenge – another stone circle similar to the one we know. They have also found a village with many small, square houses at a place nearby called Durrington Walls. This discovery was the largest Neolithic village that had ever been found in Britain. Mike's theory is that the village was where the workers lived when they were building Stonehenge 4,500 years ago. Bones and pottery fragments suggest that the workers were among the very first farming communities in Britain. They used to cook their meat over an open fire in the centre of the house and the people living in the village also had regular feasts.

Thanks to the findings of Mike's team, we now know much more about prehistoric life. The research continues to give us regular new evidence of what life was like in the distant past, why people went to such great trouble to build Stonehenge and what it was used for. A road and river route from the stone circles to a similar wooden construction at Durrington suggests that the Stonehenge monument was part of a much larger complex of buildings where people lived and worked, and not a single, separate building. We are now closer than ever before to solving the puzzle of this mysterious site.

Mike Parker Pearson has written or co-written 14 books, including *The Archaeology of Death and Burial* and *The English Heritage Book of Bronze Age Britain*. He is a regular and popular guest on many television programmes.

1 Read the article and choose the correct answers, a, b or c.

1 Mike's interest in archaeology began
- **a** because his grandfather taught him about it.
- **b** around the age of 14.
- **c** after a discovery in his own garden.

2 Mike has been working at Stonehenge
- **a** since he was 14.
- **b** for four years.
- **c** since 2003.

3 Bluestonehenge was
- **a** another name for Stonehenge.
- **b** like Stonehenge.
- **c** the name of the village.

4 The village that Mike uncovered
- **a** was very big.
- **b** was small.
- **c** is now used for homes for workers.

5 The remains found in the village tell us about
- **a** farming methods.
- **b** cooking methods.
- **c** farming and cooking methods.

6 As a result of Mike's work, we now believe that the original stone circle
- **a** was not the only building.
- **b** had a road through it.
- **c** had people living in it.

2 Choose the correct meanings as they are used in the text.

1	sparked (2)	started / made a small fire
2	dig (2)	prepare the earth for growing food / a project
3	took part (2)	helped / directed
4	communities (3)	groups of people / groups of animals
5	feasts (3)	daily meals / large celebrations
6	findings (4)	ideas / discoveries
7	evidence (4)	what helps us learn / what the police look for
8	the distant past (4)	not long ago / a long time ago
9	construction (4)	building / road
10	solving (4)	finding the answer to / asking questions about

3 Talk about one or more of the following questions with a partner.

- What do you know about the people who lived in your country thousands of years ago?
- Which archaeological sites do you know about? What are they famous for?
- Have you ever thought about becoming an archaeologist? What would be good or bad about the job?
- How helpful is it for us to understand the past?

NATIONAL GEOGRAPHIC

Careers

4

> Grammar

Learn about *will*, two uses of *going to*, the present continuous for the future, and the future continuous.

> Vocabulary

Learn words for jobs, sports people and places, and clothes.

Work with adjective + *to* + infinitive combinations, and verb + noun combinations.

> Skills

Read about sports champions, careers in design, and sport in Australia.

Listen to a conversation about clothes, and the sports news.

Write about arrangements.

> Communicate

Talk about preferences.

1 Look at the photo and choose the best caption.

a The paramedics are discussing a patient.
b The engineers are checking the measurements.
c The mechanics are fixing the engine.

2 Find jobs in the vocabulary box where people:

- wear a uniform
- work outdoors
- work indoors
- use machines

accountant	electrician	paramedic
actor	engineer	postal worker
architect	lawyer	secretary
chef	manager	soldier
designer	mechanic	

3 4.1 **Listen to three people talking about their jobs. Write the numbers (1–3) next to the jobs in the vocabulary box.**

4 Tell your partner two jobs that you'd like to do and two you wouldn't like to do. Explain your reasons.

A: *I'd like to be a chef. I like cooking.*
B: *I'd like to be a secretary. I like organising things.*

4A Sporting success

Chris: Now, who can forget the Brazilian grand prix last season – it was so exciting to watch, wasn't it? Let's see those last few minutes again.

Commentator: They're nearly at the finish line. Webber is in the lead and he's going to win the race ... yes! It's Webber first, with Kubica second. But here's Button. Button only needs a few more points to win the championship. Can he do it? He's going to finish in fifth place ... there he goes across the line. Yes! It's Hamilton third, Button fifth and so he wins the championship! What a day for British racing!

Chris: Fantastic! But what's next for millionaire racing driver Jenson Button? Will he stay with Brawn or will he go to McLaren? What do you think, Alan?

Alan: Well, he's said that money isn't the key factor and I don't think he'll change his mind. He also earns a lot from advertising, of course. On the other hand, a contract with McLaren is worth £6 million a year. So it's difficult to say what he'll do.

Chris: OK, we'll come back to the glamorous world of Formula One later this afternoon, but first let's look at the career of another world champion, Beth Tweddle. Now, gymnastics doesn't make as many headlines as motor racing, so it's easy to forget that Tweddle became champion on the same day as Button.

Alan: And that gymnastics is a tough sport. Beth has had six ankle operations and she's having another operation next week. She's competing in the European Championships next year, but it's hard to imagine she'll win another medal there.

Chris: I'm not sure I agree. She trains six days a week and injuries don't stop her! She's 24 now, which is quite old for a gymnast, but she's going to carry on for as long as she can and she's definitely not going to retire until after the next Olympics.

Vocabulary: sports people and places

1 **Which sports do you associate with these people? Add four more names and test your partner.**

Robert Korzeniowski — Serena Williams
Lionel Messi — Justyna Kowalczykç

2 **Work in pairs. Put the words into two groups: *people* and *places*. What sports are played in each place?**

> coach court manager physiotherapist pitch player pool referee ring sponsor stadium track trainer umpire

3 **Complete the sentences with words from the box in Exercise 2.**

1 A .... treats sports injuries.
2 A football .... chooses the team and plans its activities.
3 A .... gives money to teams and sports people.
4 A .... or a .... makes sure athletes are fit.
5 A .... or an .... keeps the score during a sports event.

Reading and listening

4 4.2 **Read and listen to a commentary from a TV sports programme. Which sports are mentioned?**

> athletics boxing football gymnastics motor racing tennis

5 **Read the text again. Are the sentences true or false – or is there not enough information to decide?**

1. Lewis Hamilton won the grand prix race.
2. Jenson Button wants to change teams.
3. Beth Tweddle is a gymnast.
4. Beth Tweddle can't train at the moment.

Working with words: adjective + *to* + infinitive

6 **Look at the examples. Find two more similar patterns in the text.**

It was so exciting to watch.
It's difficult to say what he'll do.

See Working with words: Page 103

Grammar: the future

7 **Look at the examples (1–3). Match them with the meanings (a–c).**

1. I don't think he'll change his mind.
2. She's having another operation next week.
3. She's going to carry on for as long as she can.

a a plan or intention
b an arrangement at a specified time in the future
c a prediction

See Grammar Explorer: Page 121

8 **Complete this sentence from the text. Then choose the correct option.**

He's .... win the race.
We use *going to* / *will* to make predictions based on the situation now.

9 **Look at the pictures. Write sentences about what's going to happen. Use verbs from the box.**

beat crash fall off save score win

10 **Choose the correct option.**

1. Arsenal **will play** / **are playing** against Manchester United tomorrow.
2. Look! The referee **will give** / **is going to give** him a red card!
3. Murray **will win** / **is winning** the next game.
4. After the match, the winners **are celebrating** / **are going to celebrate**.
5. I think Bolt **will break** / **is breaking** the record again.

11 **Read an interview with an athlete and choose the correct options.**

Q: Is it true that you (**1**) .... your manager?
A: No, it isn't. I've got no intention of doing that!
Q: And (**2**) .... in the next Olympics?
A: Of course. In fact, I (**3**) .... my training programme next month.
Q: Do you think you (**4**) .... a medal?
A: Well, I hope so. I (**5**) .... my best.

1	**a**	are going to change	**b**	will change
2	**a**	are you going to compete	**b**	will you compete
3	**a**	am starting	**b**	will start
4	**a**	are winning	**b**	will win
5	**a**	am doing	**b**	am going to do

Speaking

12 **Work in groups. What are the good things or bad things about being a sports professional?**

training routine travel personal life money injury fame

Fast finishers

Which do you think is the odd one out in each list? Why? Write more lists for a partner.

1. football golf hockey rugby
2. cricket cycling motor racing running
3. badminton baseball tennis volleyball
4. boxing fencing judo skiing

4B Designing the future

Vocabulary: clothes

1 **STUDY SKILLS** **Add the words from the vocabulary box to the mind map.**

bright cotton denim dress flared
flowered hooded jacket long-sleeved
loose pastel round-neck short-sleeved
spotted tight trousers V-neck

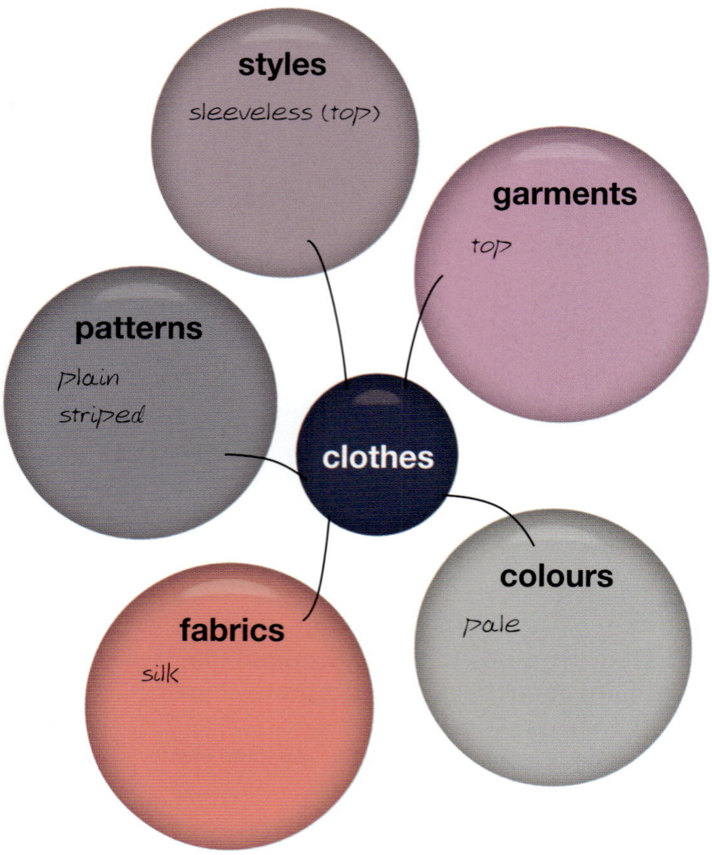

Listening

2 4.3 **Listen to two people talking about clothes. Choose the correct option (a–c).**

a They are buying clothes in a shop.
b They are choosing clothes for a party.
c They are discussing summer clothes.

3 4.3 **Listen again and choose the correct answers (a–c).**

1 Elizabeth Morris's collection
  a is brightly-coloured and patterned.
  b is plain cotton and denim.
  c has long-sleeved shirts and T-shirts.

2 Janice Spencer's collection
  a has sleeveless tops and loose trousers.
  b is in pale colours.
  c has striped and checked jackets.

Speaking

4 **Work in pairs. Describe the people in the photos using words from the vocabulary box in Exercise 1.**

5 **Choose someone in the class and describe their clothes. Can your partner identify the person? Take turns.**

Reading and listening

6 **Read the webpage quickly. What is its purpose? Choose the correct option (a–c).**

a to give advice to high-school students
b to help unemployed people to get a job
c to give information about different universities

7 4.4 **Read and listen to the webpage. Answer the questions.**

1 What kind of jobs do designers do?
2 What is CAD?
3 What do you need to get a job as a designer?

Working with words: verb + noun

8 **Look at the examples. Think of two more expressions with *get* or *have*.**

Get help from our careers files.
Perhaps you have a future as a designer.

See Working with words: Page 103

Grammar: future continuous

9 **Complete these sentences from the webpage. Which verbs do we use to make the future continuous?**

We .... new sections every week.
.... you .... or studying?

We make the negative form with *won't*:
I won't be living at home five years from now..

See Grammar Explorer: Page 122

Careers advice service

Welcome to this new service! We'll be adding new sections every week, so come back often.

Where will you be five years from now? Will you be working or studying? Will you be living with your parents or travelling the world? Decisions that you make now can affect your career choices later. Get help from our careers files. Click on the jobs to find out more.

Careers in Design

What will life in the future look like? What will the latest mobile phone be like? What will we be wearing? What kind of cars will we be driving? If these questions interest you, perhaps you have a future as a designer. Designers work in a range of fields. Most people are familiar with fashion design. Graphic designers can work in advertising, publishing, and so on. Web design is a new and popular field. Many product designers use computer programs (CAD) in their jobs.

What do I need?

You need to be good at art, of course. Designers also need to be able to express ideas visually. For example, choosing the best image for the book cover of a detective story – a picture of flowers, an abstract design, a gun? Each image will send a different message to the reader. You'll also need to get a qualification from a college or art school and build up a good portfolio. Click here for a list of courses.

10 Complete the sentences with the future continuous form of the verbs in the box. There is one extra verb.

e.g. This summer, everyone *will be wearing* pale colours.

do	drive	go	live
play	wear	work	

1. By the time I'm 25, I .... in my dream job.
2. Ten years from now, we .... electric cars.
3. This time on Sunday, I .... football.
4. What .... you .... this time tomorrow?
5. In a few months' time, we .... on holiday.

Speaking

11 Work in groups. Write sentences about your future. Don't write your name. Mix up the sentences and read them to the group. Can you guess who wrote them?

e.g. *In two / five / ten years' time, ...*

Study skills

Mind maps

1. Mind maps are a good way to help you learn new words. Look at the maps on the opposite page and on page 23. Then organise vocabulary on these topics: *animals, sport, mass media*. Choose your own sub-categories.
2. Mind maps are useful to help you plan essays. Make a mind map before you do the writing task on page 45.

4C Talking about preferences

Reading and listening

1 4.5 **Read and listen to the dialogue. What jobs do Fay, Joe and Dan want to do?**

2 Read the dialogue again and answer the questions.

1 Who wants to do media studies and art?

2 Who doesn't want to do media studies or French?

3 Find the *Useful expressions* in the dialogue. Who says each sentence?

USEFUL EXPRESSIONS

.... I'd like to drop French.
.... I want to do media studies.
.... I don't want to do French.
.... I prefer chemistry to media studies.
.... I'd rather do media studies.
.... I'd rather be in the gym than in a classroom.

4 4.6 **Listen and repeat the *Useful expressions*. Focus on your intonation.**

Fay: Oh, no. Another D for chemistry. I'm going to fail next week's test, I know.

Joe: I'll help you revise, if you like.

Fay: Thanks, but it doesn't really matter. I'm going to drop chemistry next year. I want to do media studies instead.

Joe: Really? I prefer chemistry to media studies.

Dan: Not me, I'd rather do media studies. Anyway, Fay, won't you need chemistry?

Fay: No, I don't think I will – not if I'm going to be a famous actress!

Dan: OK, so which other subjects are you going to take?

Fay: I'm not sure. It's hard to decide. I'd like to do just music and drama all the time! What about you?

Dan: I haven't got a clue. Well, I need art, obviously, to be a fashion designer. I'd like to drop French, though.

Joe: I don't want to do French either. I'd rather be in the gym than in a classroom.

Fay: And what will you do when you're an international sports star? You'll need to speak different languages, won't you?

Joe: Ah well, I'll be rich enough to have a translator by then!

Pronunciation: words with /s/ and /z/ sounds

5 4.7 **Listen to the words. Which words have an *s* sound and which have a *z* sound?**

baseball busy design disappear
fossil history instead museum
pleased presentation sponsor
thousand used *(past simple)* used to

6 4.7 **Listen and repeat the words in Exercise 5.**

Writing: arrangements

1 Read the emails and answer the questions.

1 Where are Holly and Lisa going next week?
2 Why are they going there?
3 Which day are they going there?
4 How will they find each other?

2 Complete these sentences from the emails. Which tenses are used?

1 By the time you .... this, I .... probably ....
2 Can you let me know as soon as you .... out the day of your visit?
3 I'll wait until you .... there.
4 Text me when you .... home.

See Grammar Explorer: Page 122

3 Complete the sentences with the expressions in the box. More than one answer is sometimes possible.

as soon as by the time when until

1 Can you phone me .... your sister arrives?
2 I'll text you .... the match ends.
3 I'll probably be home .... my dad hears my message.
4 I can't go home .... the bell rings.
5 .... I finish this question, the exam will be over.

4 Write a message to your partner arranging to meet. Reply to your partner's message and confirm the details. Use some of the expressions from Exercise 3. Use these ideas or ideas of your own.

a sports event a concert
a shopping trip a day trip

Speaking

7 Work in pairs. Choose the correct option (a–c). Then practise the dialogues.

1 **A:** Do you like tennis? There's a game on TV.
B: Oh, I (**1**) .... athletics, really.
A: OK, I think there's athletics on another channel.
B: Actually, I (**2**) .... read my book.

1 **a** 'd like to **b** 'd rather **c** prefer
2 **a** 'd rather **b** prefer **c** want

2 **A:** Do you prefer plain or patterned T-shirts?
B: Plain – and with long sleeves.
A: Oh, I (**1**) .... short sleeves.
B: But I (**2**) .... wear a shirt than a T-shirt, anyway.

1 **a** 'd like to **b** 'd rather **c** prefer
2 **a** 'd like to **b** 'd rather **c** prefer

8 Work in pairs. Compare your preferences. Use the dialogues in Exercise 7 to help you.

basketball football tennis	boots shoes trainers	burger pasta pizza	maths English biology

Hi Lisa,
I've just seen the list of work experience placements and I see you're going to PC World next week – so am I! If we're going to be there on the same day, we can go together. I'm not sure which day it is yet, but by the time you get this, I'll probably know. Can you let me know as soon as you find out the day of your visit?
See you
Holly

Hi Holly,
I saw your name too – we're both going to PC World on Wednesday. We can meet outside the main entrance (PC World is quite close to my house actually). I'll wait until you get there. Or you can text me when you leave home on Wednesday morning if you like.
See you then!
Lisa

4D Sport in Australia

Reading

1 **What sports do you associate with Australia? Read the text quickly and see if they are mentioned.**

2 4.8 **Read the text again. Answer the questions.**

1. What is 'Surfers Paradise'?
2. What is the 'Australian Open'?
3. Who is Ian Thorpe?
4. What is 'footy'?

3 **Find words in the text that mean the same as the underlined words.**

1. It's nice to eat outside in the summer.
2. There were 50,000 people in the audience at the tennis final.
3. There's a lot of competition between Arsenal and Chelsea.
4. The best athletes take part in the world championships.

Culture

Australia has the perfect ingredients for life outdoors – warm, sunny weather and lots of open spaces. Australians are so passionate about sport that nine of the ten most popular TV shows are about sports. But taking part is equally important.

Beach sports

As an island continent, Australia has more than 34,000 kilometres of coastline – mostly sandy beaches and the warm water of the Pacific and Indian Oceans. Almost everyone in Australia learns to swim when they are young – either at primary school, in the pool at home or at a nearby beach. Kids who live near the ocean often go surfing after school. The big surfing fashion and clothing companies sponsor the best surfers, so some people have a professional career as surfers. There's even a town in the state of Queensland called Surfers Paradise!

International events

The Formula One grand prix at Melbourne is a huge spectator event. Spectators also fill every available seat at the 'Ashes series' cricket matches. This sports rivalry between England and Australia has a long history, going back to 1882. But you can also see people playing cricket in parks and on beaches all through the summer. The Australian Open is one of the four 'grand slam' tennis tournaments. It's also the first big event of the tennis year and all the top players compete there.

The Olympic Games

Australia has hosted the Summer Olympics twice – in Melbourne in 1956 and in Sydney in 2000 – and it's one of only a few countries that has taken part in all of the summer Olympics. Swimmer Ian Thorpe won a total of nine Olympic medals, including five golds, before he retired in 2006. Australia has won Olympic medals in sports such as canoeing, water polo and beach volleyball too.

Did you know?

Make sure you know the names of sports if you go to Australia. Football is called soccer there. And they play a game which looks like rugby, but it's called Aussie Rules football or footy!

4 **Which verbs do we use with *surfing* and *cricket*? Check in the text. Then put these sports into two groups.**

beach volleyball canoeing football rugby swimming tennis water polo

Listening

5 4.9 **Listen to the sports news. Are the sentences true or false?**

1 Snow has affected many sports events.
2 Wayne Rooney will be playing in the next Champions League match.
3 France has won the Six Nations rugby championship.
4 The British athletics team is top of the medals table in Glasgow.
5 Roger Federer is launching a new fashion collection.

6 4.9 **Listen again and choose the correct option (a–c).**

1 Wayne Rooney has a .... injury.
 a foot
 b head
 c knee
2 France beat .... in the last Six Nations game.
 a England
 b Ireland
 c Scotland
3 Venus Williams has her own .... label.
 a clothing
 b jewellery
 c perfume

Project

Write a short text about sport in your country. Find some photos in a magazine or on the Internet. Use the questions to help you.

- Do people prefer outdoor or indoor sports?
- What sports are popular after-school activities?
- What kind of international events are held?
- What are your national sports?

Physics and English

Newton's laws of motion

1 **Read the text and answer the questions.**

1 What's the scientific word that describes 'pushing' or 'pulling'?
2 What's another word for 'movement'?
3 What's the name of the force that pulls things to the Earth?

Sir Isaac Newton (1642–1727) was an English physicist. He described some of the basic laws of nature. These laws are known as 'Newton's laws of motion' and 'Newton's law of universal gravitation'.

We can see these laws in action when we watch sports. Imagine the world champion ski jumper, Lindsey Van, at the top of a ski jump. She is waiting to jump and she is standing still. She won't begin to move until she pushes herself forward. A push, or a pull, is called a 'force' in physics. Then, when Van pushes forward, she starts to move down the ski jump. She doesn't need to push now. This is Newton's first law of motion. It says that objects stay still if there is no force. It also says that objects keep moving in the same direction until they meet another force.

Van reaches the end of the ski jump and takes off into the air. But she doesn't continue in the same direction – flying through the air – forever, because she meets another force. The most important force in action here is gravity. Gravity pulls everything towards the centre of the Earth, and that means it pulls Van towards the ground. But she falls slowly, not instantly. Why? This is because while her body pushes down on the air, the air also pushes her up. It's Newton's third law of motion: forces act in pairs.

2 **Read the text again and decide if these sentences about Newton's first law of motion are true or false.**

1 An object won't move unless something pushes or pulls it.
2 A moving object won't stop if there is no force against it.

3 **Can you think of other examples which demonstrate Newton's laws? Compare with your partner.**

Consolidation Units 3 and 4

Reading

Identifying the main idea

- Read the whole text quickly without worrying about words you don't understand.
- Decide what you think the main topic of the text is and look for this in the options in the task.
- Read the text again to confirm your choice and to make sure that the alternatives are not correct.
- **Important!** You need to read the whole text to find the main idea.

1 Read the text and find the key words. What do you think the topic of the text is?

Not everybody has the talent to be a professional sportsperson, but there's a variety of jobs you can do – from being an instructor to being a professional referee. You need to be good at sports, of course, and for most jobs you'll need a qualification. You'll also need excellent 'people skills'.

2 Which option (a–c) matches your answer to Exercise 1?

a Sports celebrities
b Studying sport
c Careers in sport

3 Read the text and choose the correct option (a–c).

I love fashion and I want to be a fashion designer. There's a course at my local college, so I'm going to apply for a place there. It's a three-year course and with that qualification, I'll be able to work in one of the big fashion companies. I'll probably move to London, which will be quite exciting, or even Paris! I know that it's a difficult career, but I'm going to work really hard to succeed. In 2020, someone will be wearing one of my designs to the Oscars!

The text is about the writer's … .

a designs
b experience
c plans

Grammar

Choosing the correct word form

- Read the whole text quickly.
- Look at the gapped sentences. What kind of words are missing?
- Look at the options given for each gap. Choose the option that matches the grammar and logic of the gapped sentence.
- **Important!** Try each option before you decide.

1 Look at the words in each group. Are they nouns, verbs, adjectives or pronouns?

1 amazed frightening brilliant
2 buy play go
3 that which who
4 do have will

2 What kind of word is missing from each gap?

1 We .... never seen such a brilliant athlete!
2 What time are you .... to the party?
3 It wasn't a very good match. It was a bit ....
4 This is the race .... is the most important.

3 Look at the options for each gap in Exercise 2. Choose the correct answers.

1	**a**	has	**b**	have	**c**	having
2	**a**	going	**b**	go	**c**	went
3	**a**	boring	**b**	bore	**c**	bored
4	**a**	who	**b**	what	**c**	which

4 Read the text and choose the correct option (a–c).

Hi Dan,

We've got tickets for the Cup Final next month! I'm so (**1**) .... ! Do you want to come with us? It's on Saturday 11th and (**2**) .... leaving at about 6 a.m. I know it's really early, but my dad thinks it (**3**) .... us about four hours to get there. I'd love you to come – and you don't have to pay for the ticket either!
(**4**) .... call you later.

Joe

1	**a** excite	**b** excited	**c** exciting
2	**a** we'll	**b** we're	**c** we've
3	**a** takes	**b** is taking	**c** will take
4	**a** I'm	**b** I'd	**c** I'll

Verb + -*ing*

We use verb + -*ing* after certain verbs such as *avoid, enjoy, finish, imagine, mind, recommend, suggest, stop.*

Jojo really enjoys eating bananas.

1 Complete the sentences with the correct form of the verbs in the box.

avoid	**finish**	**imagine**
mind	**recommend**	**stop**

1 Superstitious people .... opening umbrellas in the house.
2 Have you .... reading that book yet?
3 The show is very popular, so I .... buying tickets in advance.
4 I can't .... being hypnotised.
5 Please .... whistling! It's very annoying.
6 'Sorry, I'm not ready yet.' 'It's OK. I don't .... waiting.'

A verb which follows a preposition ends in -*ing*.

Mark's great at fixing things.

2 Match the beginnings of the sentences (1–5) with the endings (a–e).

1 English people are famous for
2 You can improve your English by
3 Are you afraid of
4 What did Jensen Button do after
5 I'm not really interested in

a flying?
b playing games or doing sports.
c practising every day.
d talking about the weather.
e winning the Formula One championship?

We use verb + -*ing* as the subject of a sentence.

Looking for UFOs is a waste of time.

3 Complete the sentences with the -*ing* form of the verbs. Make as many sentences as you can.

act	**dance**	**meet**
perform	**see**	**sing**

1 .... in a competition is terrifying.
2 .... in front of an audience feels amazing.
3 .... my idol was fantastic.

to + infinitive

We use *to* + infinitive after verbs such as *agree, decide, want* and after adjectives such as *easy, impossible, pleased.*

See Working with words: Page 102.

Begin, continue, hate, like, love, start can be followed by both *to* + infinitive and verb + -*ing*. The meaning is the same. The meaning is different with other verbs such as *try*.

4 How many verbs from the box can you use to complete each sentence?

begin	**continue**	**hate**	**like**
love	**start**		

1 I really .... eating chocolate cake.
2 OK, you can .... to fry the sausages now.
3 When did you .... learning English?
4 She says she'll .... to do lots of sport when she leaves school.

5 Write the verb in the correct form.

1 I'm quite excited about .... (**go**) on holiday.
2 I'm pleased .... (**meet**) you, Mr Jones.
3 The league has decided .... (**cancel**) the match.
4 Do you enjoy .... (**cook**)?
5 .... (**make**) dinner for ten people is hard work.

Review Units 3 and 4

Vocabulary

1 Write the words.

1 sixty seconds = ...
2 100 years = ...
3 two weeks = ...
4 ten years = ...
5 sixty minutes = ...

1 mark per item: .../5 marks

2 Write the jobs.

1 ....
2 ....
3 ....
4 ....
5 ....

1 mark per item: .../5 marks

3 Complete the sports places.

1 a swimming p............
2 a racing t............
3 a football p............
4 a boxing r............
5 a tennis c............

1 mark per item: .../5 marks

4 Match the words (1–5) with the categories (a–e).

1	cotton, silk	a	patterns
2	bright, pastel	b	garments
3	a skirt, a top	c	fabrics
4	hooded, V-neck	d	styles
5	striped, plain	e	colours

1 mark per item: .../5 marks

5 Write the American English word that means the same as the British English word.

1 holiday = ...
2 flat = ...
3 shop = ...
4 biscuit = ...
5 chips = ...

1 mark per item: .../5 marks

Grammar

6 Complete the sentences with the past simple or past perfect form of the verbs.

1 I was late. The lesson .... (**start**).
2 After you left, I .... (**go**) home.
3 Tests showed that the animal .... (**not / live**) very long.
4 I couldn't call you because I .... (**not / write down**) your number.
5 The man .... (**see**) a robbery and called the police.

1 mark per item: .../5 marks

7 Make statements and questions with *used to*.

1 Which cartoons / you / watch?
2 I / love / Bugs Bunny.
3 they / read / comics?
4 We / not like / cheese.
5 My brother / cry / a lot.

1 mark per item: .../5 marks

8 Complete the sentences with the present continuous or *going to* form of the verb.

1 Look at Rooney! He .... (**score**)!
2 I've decided I .... (**work / hard**).
3 Chelsea .... (**play**) Milan tonight.
4 What a win! The fans .... (**be**) pleased.
5 What time .... we .... (**meet**) on Friday?

1 mark per item: .../5 marks

9 Is the future continuous correct in each sentence?

1 This summer, we**'ll be wearing** lots of red and blue.
2 This time next week, we**'ll be watching** the final.
3 Do you think you**'ll be liking** university?
4 In a month's time, I**'ll be doing** my final exams.
5 I think he**'ll be winning** the race.

1 mark per item: .../5 marks

10 Write the verb in the correct form.

1 I'm worried about .... (**take**) the test.
2 It's easy .... (**lose**) against that team.
3 Did you enjoy .... (**meet**) the Queen?
4 .... (**wait**) for the results of an exam is always horrible.
5 Did you learn .... (**speak**) French at school?

1 mark per item: .../5 marks

Communicate

11 Complete the questions.

1 .... does it take to fry an egg?
2 .... people live in your house?
3 .... is it from London to Manchester?
4 .... money have you got?
5 .... was the last Ice Age?

2 marks per item: .../10 marks

12 Complete the dialogue with the expressions.

do you want **I don't want** **I prefer** **I'd like** **I'd rather**

Dad: What (**1**) .... for lunch today?
Mum: Oh, I don't know.
Kate: (**2**) .... sausage and chips, please.
Dad: Oh, no. We had that the other day. (**3**) .... to have it again.
Mum: Well, (**4**) .... go out than eat at home.
Dad: No, we're not going out. You can have pasta or sandwiches.
Kate: Well (**5**) .... sandwiches to pasta.
Dad: OK, sandwiches.

2 marks per item: .../10 marks

13 Does the *s* in these words sound like /s/ or /z/?

1 busy ....
2 design ....
3 disappear ....
4 fossil ....
5 museum ....
6 newspaper ....
7 pleased ....
8 roasting ....
9 sausage ....
10 thousand ....

2 marks per item: .../10 marks

14 Rewrite the sentences with *that* and *so* or *such*.

1 I was tired. I had to sit down. (**so**)
2 It was a hard exam. I couldn't do it. (**such**)
3 The stadium was full. We couldn't get in. (**so**)
4 It was a boring game. I fell asleep. (**such**)
5 My friend was thirsty. He drank three cans of cola. (**so**)

2 marks per item: .../10 marks

15 Complete the email with these words.

as **at** **if** **next** **not** **them** **to** **until** **when** **will**

Here are the arrangements for (**1**) .... Saturday. Please read (**2**) .... carefully. I don't want anyone (**3**) .... miss the trip!

Please give your name to me as soon (**4**) .... you arrive and then get on the bus. (**5**) .... everyone is on the bus, we (**6**) .... leave. However, if you aren't there by eight o'clock, we will (**7**) .... wait.

After we set off, there will be no stops (**8**) .... we arrive at the stadium. (**9**) .... there are any questions, please email me immediately. See you all (**10**) .... 8 a.m. on Saturday!

1 mark per item: .../10 marks

Total: .../100

I can...

I can talk about quantity, time and distance.
I can talk about preferences.

PROJECT Talking about the future

1 Read the predictions from the article and complete the gaps.

1 I think Spain .... win the European Championships.
2 I think Uruguay .... do well.
3 Jenson Button and Lewis Hamilton .... beat Mark Webber.
4 The summer collections .... out in the next couple of months.
5 I think we .... see some major changes in clothes.
6 In five years' time, I think we .... the end of denim.
7 By 2020, I don't think we .... the same kind of clothes.
8 I think they .... invent new fabrics.
9 Fifty years from now, we .... wear loose clothing to stay cool.
10 The world .... change and it's difficult to say exactly how.
11 I don't think the jobs today .... available.
12 I'm sure we .... new skills.
13 Machines .... the work in the future.
14 There .... a demand for some jobs.
15 People .... keep up-to-date with the latest developments.

2 With a partner, discuss these questions.

- Who do you think is going to win the next Formula One Championship / tennis tournament / basketball championship, etc)?
- Which sports will become more/less popular?
- What will people be wearing this summer / in five years' time / 50 years from now?
- Do you think any of the things we wear today will disappear in the future?
- What kind of jobs and skills will/won't we need in the future?
- Do you think people will earn more or less money than today?

3 Make notes about *your* future. Use phrases like those below. Compare notes with a partner.

I will probably … I'd like to …
I want to … I'd rather …
I'm going to …

What's going to happen?

Angela Brown continues her series of predictions for the future.

Sport

I think Spain are going to win the European Championship. It's possible that one of the South American teams will win the next World Cup. I think Uruguay will probably do well again. In Formula One, Jenson Button and Lewis Hamilton will need to beat Mark Webber, who I think is going to be the next champion.

Clothes

The summer collections are coming out in the next couple of months, and everyone is excited. But, looking further ahead, I think we are going to see some major changes in the clothes we wear. In five years' time, I think we will finally see the end of denim. And, looking further ahead, by 2020, I don't think we will be wearing the same styles, and I think they will invent new fabrics. Fifty years from now, I think we will all have to wear loose clothing, with long-sleeved tops and perhaps flared trousers, to cover up from the sun and to stay cool.

Careers

The world is going to change, and it's difficult to say exactly how. I don't think the jobs that are out there today will be available in a few years and I'm sure we'll have to learn new skills as the job market changes. I think people will have to learn how to use new machines but, mostly, I think the machines will be doing the work in the future. We'll just be watching them to make sure they don't break down. But there will always be a demand for some jobs – we'll always need doctors, paramedics, mechanics and accountants, for example. But people are going to have to keep up-to-date with the latest developments because – and this is my last prediction – things are going to be changing fast!

Project

Write about your predictions for the future.

- Choose one of the headings: **Clothes / Sport / Careers**
- Write about what you think *will / is going to* happen
- Add one heading called **Me** and write about your future
- When you write about yourself, you can use *I'd like to, I want to* and *I'd rather* for the future
- You can also use the future continuous or the present continuous for the future
- Don't forget to use the vocabulary from Unit 4
- Try to find interesting pictures showing now or the future (or draw your own)

Special things

5

> Grammar

Learn about the present simple, past simple, present continuous, past continuous, present perfect passive, and the passive with modal verbs: *can, must, will.*

> Vocabulary

Learn words for materials, and adjectives for size and shape.

Work with adjective order, and verb + preposition combinations.

> Skills

Read about the New Seven Wonders of the World, gold, and natural resources in Canada.

Listen to a story from Greek mythology, and some statistics about Canada.

Write a description of an object.

> Communicate

Express purpose and give reasons.

1 **Work in pairs. How many of the materials in the vocabulary box can you see in the photo?**

brick	glass	paper	stone
concrete	leather	plastic	wood
fabric	metal	rubber	wool

2 **What are these things made of? Use words from the vocabulary box.**

books	bottles	cars
clothes	computers	school desks
shoes	skyscrapers	toothbrushes

3 5.1 **Listen to two conversations. Answer the questions. Can you identify the objects?**

1 How big is it?
2 What's it made of?
3 What's it for?

4 **Work in pairs. Choose four objects each. Ask and answer questions about your objects and discover your partner's objects.**

5A World wonders

Win a Wonderful Holiday for Two!

In 2007, the New Seven Wonders of the World were chosen. Win our competition and you can visit one of these remarkable places – just write and tell us which continent each 'Wonder' is in.

The Taj Mahal, Agra, India

Many people imagine that the Taj Mahal was built as a palace. In fact, it is a beautiful tomb, designed by an Indian ruler Shah Jahan, to commemorate his wife. It took more than 20 years to build. The immense white marble blocks were pulled into position by 1,000 elephants.

The Great Wall of China

The wall was constructed to keep out China's enemies. Sections of the ancient brick structure have been damaged by the weather and earthquakes, but it's still the largest human-made structure in the world.

Petra, Jordan

The magnificent pink-coloured rock city of Petra was carved out of a limestone mountain. Two thousand years ago it was a wealthy, busy market city at the crossroads of important trade routes. These days, it is visited by so many tourists that parts of it are being eroded.

WIN A WONDERFUL HOLIDAY FOR TWO

The Colosseum, Rome, Italy

The spectacular Colosseum has featured in films, music videos and fashion shows. It was even recreated digitally in the film *Gladiator*. That seems appropriate – it was being used for entertainment in 100 A.D. too!

Chichén Itzá, Mexico

This enormous stone city was abandoned 1,000 years ago. Maya treasure has been found there and many of the ruins are being restored today.

Machu Picchu, Peru

It takes four days to hike up to the mysterious city of Machu Picchu, 2,350 metres above sea level. Why did the Incas choose such a remote place? How were the massive granite stones moved? There are many questions that haven't been answered yet.

Christ the Redeemer, Rio de Janeiro, Brazil

This huge concrete and stone statue was erected in 1931 to celebrate 100 years of independence from Portugal. It stands on a mountain 704 metres high, above the Atlantic coast. Although it was struck by lightning in 2008, it wasn't damaged.

Reading and listening

1 **Work in pairs. Where are the two places in the photos? How much do you know about them?**

2 5.2 **Read and listen to the text. Check your answers to Exercise 1.**

3 **Read the text again. Copy and complete the table for the other six Wonders of the World. Some information isn't in the text.**

Name	Location	Material	Reason
Taj Mahal	India	marble	to commemorate a ruler's wife

4 **Which of the seven Wonders of the World would you like to visit? Why?**

Working with words: adjective order

5 **Look at the examples. Find similar adjective groups in the text.**

immense white marble blocks

ancient brick structure

See Working with words: Page 104

Grammar: passive

6 Look at the example. How do we make the passive?

In 2007, the New Seven Wonders of the World were chosen.

See Grammar Explorer: Page 123

7 Complete the table with the words in the box.

are been being being has is was was

Simple tenses	
present	Petra (**1**) .... visited by too many tourists.
past	It (**2**) .... carved out of rock.
Continuous tenses	
present	Parts of it (**3**) .... (**4**) .... eroded.
past	It (**5**) .... (**6**) .... used for entertainment.
Present perfect	
	Maya treasure (**7**) .... (**8**) .... found there.

We make the negative form by adding *n't* to *be* or *have*: *It wasn't damaged. The questions haven't been answered.*

8 Look at the example. Then complete the questions. Use the text to help you.

How were the massive granite stones moved?

1. 'When .... Chichén Itzá .... ?' 'A thousand years ago.'
2. 'Why .... parts of Petra .... ?' 'Because there are so many tourists these days.'
3. 'Why .... the Great Wall of China .... ?' 'To keep out China's enemies.'
4. 'How .... sections of the Great Wall of China .... ?'
   'By the weather and earthquakes.'

9 Rewrite each active sentence in the passive.

e.g. 20,000 workers built the Taj Mahal.
The Taj Mahal was built by 20,000 workers.

1. They completed the Taj Mahal in the 1650s.
2. People have stolen bricks from the Great Wall of China.
3. They are stopping some visits to Petra.
4. The Romans were exploiting the gladiators.
5. They didn't accept the first plans for the statue.
6. Nobody has discovered all the Chichén Itzá treasure yet.

10 Look at your sentences for Exercise 9. Write questions as in the example.

e.g. Who? *Who was the Taj Mahal built by?*

1	When?	**3**	Where?	**5**	What?
2	What?	**4**	Who?	**6**	What?

11 Write the verbs in the correct active and passive forms.

You'll need an up-to-date passport in order to travel to see your 'Wonder'. Passports (**1**) .... (**use**) for centuries, although only very important travellers (**2**) .... (**have**) them originally. In the past, passports (**3**) .... (**sign**) by a country's ruler! In the 1800s, travel for pleasure (**4**) .... (**become**) so popular in Europe that passports (**5**) .... (**abandon**) by several countries. These days, passports (**6**) .... (**change**). Data chips (**7**) .... (**introduce**) in some countries. And in the EU, passports for pets (**8**) .... (**need**) too!

Vocabulary: size and shape

12 Put the adjectives into two groups: *size* and *shape*. Divide the first group into *big* and *small*.

enormous huge immense little massive microscopic oval rectangular round square tiny triangular

13 Choose the correct option.

1. Inca roads were made of **microscopic** / **rectangular** stones.
2. Bacteria are **immense** / **tiny** organisms.
3. The Colosseum is **huge** / **oval** in shape.
4. Pyramids usually have a **square** / **round** base.
5. Data chips contain **triangular** / **massive** amounts of information.

Fast finishers

How many materials can you think of for each use?

building clothes household objects

5B Gold fever

Gold

Gold is special in every culture in the world. But why has this shiny yellow metal always been valued as a fabulous treasure?

Firstly, it's soft and dense, so it's easy to shape. It can be made into fine threads, flat sheets or intricate shapes. A great variety of both decorative and functional things can be created from gold. Secondly, it never loses its shine. This means that beautiful gold objects from centuries ago will always be treasured. And thirdly, it's extremely rare. All the gold that has ever been mined would only fill two Olympic-sized swimming pools.

Gold has been discovered in different times and places in our history. Each time, the people who owned it became rich and powerful – for example, the Incas and the Aztecs in the Americas, or the Egyptian and Mali Empires in Africa. Their gold was exchanged for other valuable goods such as Arabic horses, luxurious silk and exotic spices from places as far away as China. In the 19th century, there were gold rushes in California, South Africa and southeast Australia.

Gold can be found in rivers or mined from the ground. Most of the time it must be separated from the rock before it can be used, but occasionally large solid pieces, called nuggets, are discovered. The biggest nugget ever found weighed 72 kilograms and measured 61 x 31 centimetres.

About 60 per cent of the world's gold is turned into jewellery, but it's also used in dentistry, communications, computer and space technology and medicine. Doctors think a cancer treatment, using gold, will be developed this century.

Speaking

1 Work in pairs. What connects these things? Explain your answer.

a wedding ring	Olympic first-place medal
the Oscar statuette	50-year anniversaries

Reading and listening

2 Work in pairs. Can you guess the answers to these questions?

1. How much gold is there in the world?
2. What's a nugget?
3. Apart from jewellery, what other things is gold used for?

3 STUDY SKILLS Read the text quickly to find the answers to Exercise 2.

4 5.3 **Read and listen to the text. Based on the information in the text, do you think these sentences are true or false?**

1 Gold is a useful metal.
2 Gold can be made artificially.
3 Gold is poisonous to humans.

Working with words: verb + preposition

5 **Look at the examples. Find eight more verb + preposition combinations in the text.**

But why has this shiny yellow metal always been valued as a fabulous treasure?

It can be made into fine threads.

See Working with words: Page 104

Grammar: passive with modal verbs

6 **Look at the text and complete the sentences.**

Modal verbs	
can	It (**1**) .... (**2**) .... made into fine threads.
must	It (**3**) .... (**4**) .... separated from the rock.
will	A cancer treatment (**5**) .... (**6**) .... developed this century.

See Grammar Explorer: Page 123

7 **Look at the examples. Then write the question and negative forms of the sentences in Exercise 6.**

Can gold be made artificially?

Gold can't be made artificially.

8 **Rewrite the sentences in the passive. Begin with the underlined words.**

e.g. It's possible to shape <u>gold</u> easily.
Gold can be shaped easily.

1 It's possible to make <u>jewellery</u> from many materials.
2 It's necessary to clean <u>this ring</u> carefully.
3 It's not possible to repair <u>these earrings</u>.
4 They will announce <u>the Oscar winners</u> tonight.
5 It's necessary to keep <u>the results</u> secret.

Listening

9 5.4 **Listen to a story from Greek mythology. Choose the correct option.**

1 Match the names (1–3) with their roles (a–c).
   1 Dionysus — **a** a king
   2 Midas — **b** a servant
   3 Silenus — **c** a god
2 Midas asked for
   a payment in gold.
   b everything he touched to become gold.
   c Dionysis to make him a god.
3 Midas's daughter
   a ate some fruit and became ill.
   b hurt her hand.
   c turned into gold.
4 According to the myth, there is gold in the river Pactolus because
   a Midas bathed there.
   b Dionysus swam there.
   c the river is magic.

Speaking

10 **Work in groups. Discuss the statements. Do you think they are true or are they myths?**

1 The Great Wall of China can be seen from the moon.
2 The common cold can be cured with antibiotics.
3 Hyperactivity is caused by too much sugar.
4 Hiccups can be cured by standing on your head.
5 Vampires can't be killed.

Study skills

Scanning and skimming

1 You can improve your reading skills if you read with a purpose.
- Looking through a text quickly to find specific information, e.g. the answers to questions, times, dates, specific words. This is called scanning.
- Looking at a text to decide what it is about, if it interests you or if it is useful. This is called skimming.

2 Which technique did you use on the *Gold* text? Use the same technique when you read the text in Workbook Unit 5.

5C Expressing purpose and reasons

Reading and listening

1 5.5 **Read and listen to the dialogue. Why is Fay having a 'make-over'?**

a to change her hair colour
b because she's meeting an agent
c for a photo

2 **Read again. Are the sentences true or false? Find the information that tells you.**

1 Fay is painting her nails.
2 Holly's aunt is going to take Fay's photo.
3 Fay's hair is shorter than before.
4 Joe's dad is going to fix their computer.

See Grammar Explorer: Page 123

3 **Find the *Useful expressions* in the dialogue.**

USEFUL EXPRESSIONS

Asking about purpose and reason
What for?
What do you need a portfolio for?
Why are you going to do that?
Explaining purpose and reason
Because I need a favour.
For my photo.
So that they can promote you.
To send to agencies.

4 5.6 **Listen and repeat the *Useful expressions*. Focus on your intonation.**

Joe: Hi … oh! What's going on here?
Fay: I'm having my face done and my nails painted.
Joe: What for?
Fay: For my photo, of course.
Joe: Which photo? What are you talking about?
Holly: She's getting her photo taken for her portfolio. My aunt Lucy is a professional photographer – we're going to her studio this afternoon.
Joe: What do you need a portfolio for?
Fay: To send to agencies.
Joe: And why are you going to do that?
Fay: Because if you want to be an actor, you need an agent to find work for you! And an agent needs to have your details so that they can promote you.
Joe: Oh, I get it. Like models?
Fay: Yes, a bit. Do you like my hair?
Joe: Erm, what's different about it? Have you had it cut?
Fay: No, I've had it dyed. It's a bit darker now. Honestly!
Holly: What did you come round for, Joe, by the way?
Joe: Oh, well, actually, because I need a favour. I'd like to use your computer, if that's OK. Ours isn't working. I'm waiting for dad to get it fixed.
Holly: No problem. We're going to be busy all morning!

5 Look at the *Useful expressions* and complete the sentence in four different ways.

Joe needs a computer ...

1 .... do his homework.

2 .... he can do his homework.

3 .... his homework.

4 .... he has to do his homework.

6 5.7 **Listen to the phone messages. First, complete the missing information. Then choose the correct option.**

1 Holly wants to borrow Fay's .... **because she's going out / to wear in a photo**.

2 Fay can't meet them at the .... She's going to London **for an interview / so she can meet her aunt**.

3 Dan wants borrow Joe's .... **for the match / because he's lost his**.

Speaking

7 Work in pairs. Match the words in group 1 and the verbs in group 2. How many combinations can you make?

	1	2
have/get (your)	bedroom ears eyes hair head nose tongue	cut dyed painted pierced tested shaved

8 Ask and answer questions using the expressions.

A: *Would you like to get your nose pierced?*

B: *No, I wouldn't. What about you?*

Pronunciation: the letter 'o' and the vowel sounds /əʊ/ and /ʌ/

9 5.8 **Does the '*o*' in these words sound like the *o* in *gold* /əʊ/ or *some* /ʌ/? Listen and put them into two groups.**

above chosen clothes come done erode nose other oval own remote show stone won wonder

Writing: a description of an object

1 Read about Joe's favourite possession. Answer the questions.

1 What is it?

2 Where is it from?

3 What is it made of?

4 What is it like?

2 Look at the words in red. Which option (a–d) can be used instead of them?

a because

b for

c so that

d to

3 Rewrite the pairs of sentences with *as*, *because* and *since*.

1 My camera is digital. I don't need film.

2 My bike is easy to ride. It's got lots of gears.

3 My watch is waterproof. I can wear it when I go diving.

4 I don't wear earrings. I haven't had my ears pierced.

4 Write about your favourite possession. Use Joe's description to help you.

My most treasured possession is an old camera. It used to belong to my grandfather. He gave this object to me a few years ago because I'm interested in photography. It was made in the USA about 50 years ago and it's made of a kind of black plastic. It's a very simple, square-shaped camera and it used film. As they don't make the film now, I can't take photos with it. My grandfather used it to photograph all his friends and family. I've got some of the photos, but since he didn't write any names on them, we don't know who they are! Now I keep the camera in a cupboard so that it doesn't get damaged.

5D Boom-town Canada

Reading

1 **Work in pairs. Look at the photos of an industrial town in Canada. Which natural resource is being worked with?**

animals coal fish land minerals oil
trees water

2 **Read the text quickly and check your answer to Exercise 1. Tick the other natural resources that are mentioned.**

3 5.9 **Read the text again. How have natural resources been important in Canadian life?**

4 **What do you think the expression 'boom town' means?**

5 **Find three expressions with *get* in the text that mean the same as the underlined words.**

1 Lots of people want to <u>make a lot of money</u>.
2 We try to <u>escape</u> from city life at weekends.
3 The men went to London to <u>find work</u>.

Culture

Canada is the second largest country in the world, but it only has 0.5 per cent of the world's population. Canadian lakes and rivers contain one fifth of all the fresh water on Earth and there are vast areas of forest and open land. The fish, animals and trees from these areas have always been extremely important to Inuit communities across Canada.

These natural resources also brought many Europeans to Canada in the 17th and 18th centuries. Then, in 1896, gold was discovered in the Yukon. This changed the lives of thousands of people. Men from the USA, South Africa and Australia rushed to the area to seek their fortune. In two years, a fishing camp on the Klondike River turned into Dawson City, with a population of more than 40,000. The men were not only miners, but also doctors, teachers and other professionals. Many women also travelled there to get away from their traditional, restricted lives. Although they had to work in typical jobs like cooking and nursing, it was a new life of opportunity and adventure.

These days, Canada's boom towns are in Alberta, where oil has been found. It's easy to understand why oil is often called 'black gold'. Workers from over 70 countries have moved there to get well-paid jobs in the oil industry. Many of them live in tiny rooms in work camps. Just like in the Klondike gold rush, there are lots of opportunities. As you don't have to be physically strong to operate the 'high-tech' machinery used in the oil fields, the giant-sized vehicles are often driven by women. These trucks move more than a million tons of material every day. The women, like most of the oil workers in Alberta, hope to get rich quickly and then go home.

Listening

6 How do you say these numbers? How are they written in the text?

0.5% | 1/5
forty thousand | seventy
1,000,000

7 5.10 Listen to the statistics about Canada's natural resources. Choose the correct option (a–c).

1 The amount of mined gold in the world is .... tons.
 a 160
 b 16,000
 c 160,000
2 The amount of gold mined in the Yukon was .... tons.
 a 190
 b 390
 c 3,900
3 The population of the Yukon today is .... of Dawson City's gold-rush population.
 a ¾
 b ⅔
 c ¼
4 Alberta produces .... barrels of oil a day.
 a 12 million
 b 0.12 millon
 c 1.2 million
5 The USA gets .... of its oil from Canada.
 a 9 per cent
 b 19 per cent
 c 90 per cent

UK	Europe
1,000,000	1.000.000
1.5	1,5

Project

Work in groups. Choose at least twelve things you use or consume every day – clothes, objects, food, etc. Find or make a large map of the world and show where the things come from.

Chemistry and English

Elements

1 Find out about elements. Read the text and answer the questions.

1 What are elements made of?
2 What are some examples of elements?
3 What happens when elements are mixed together?

Gold is an element. Elements are pure materials. An element can't be separated into different materials. It is made of identical atoms. Atoms are so tiny that you can't see them.

Most elements are solid at room temperature. Examples of solid elements are gold, silver, carbon, copper and aluminium. A few elements are gases at room temperature, for example oxygen, hydrogen and nitrogen. Some elements can be mixed together to make 'compounds'. For example, hydrogen and oxygen together form a very common compound: water. Another common compound is made of the two elements sodium and chlorine: salt.

silver

gold

copper

carbon

Elements can be divided into two groups, metals and non-metals. Most elements are metals. Metals are shiny and strong but can be bent quite easily. They also conduct electricity and heat. Gold is a typical metal. Non-metals include solid elements and gases. Solid non-metals are not shiny or strong and they break easily.

Each element is known by a chemical symbol, as well as its name. This is always written the same way and it's the same in every language of the world:

aluminium	**Al**	hydrogen	**H**
carbon	**C**	nitrogen	**N**
copper	**Cu**	oxygen	**O**
gold	**Au**	silver	**Ag**

2 What are the two main groups of elements and what are their properties?

3 Why is it a good idea to use chemical symbols instead of names?

TRUE STORY

Searching for gold

1 What do you know about gold? Discuss these questions with a partner before you read the article:

1 Where does gold come from?
2 What is a gold rush?
3 What methods do people use in order to look for gold?
4 How do we get most of our gold?

2 Read the first section of the article and answer the questions.

1 What do you understand by the phrase 'flooded into the area'?
2 What does it mean when we say 'prospect' for gold?
3 Who was a 'forty-niner'?
4 What happened in San Francisco.
5 What happened to the forty-niners.

3 Now read the rest of the article and find a word or phrase that means the following.

1 people who like something (1)
2 do something on your own (2)
3 really; seriously (2)
4 kind; keen to help (3)
5 pieces of advice (3)
6 walking in the country (3)

Gold rush

In 1848, James W Marshall discovered gold in California. The following year, around 300,000 people flooded into the area to search or 'prospect' for gold. They were often called 'forty-niners' after the year – 1849.

Before the discovery, San Francisco had a population of around 500 people, but this number rose to around 150,000 in just over 20 years. The city grew rapidly, but most of the gold was found by large companies. The original forty-niners, most of whom hadn't got rich, had to find work somewhere else.

In recent years, there has been a new gold rush. Thousands of enthusiasts in the US go looking for gold at the weekends or during their summer holidays.

One of those enthusiasts is Chris Ralph. He is a modern-day gold prospector who has been involved in the search for gold in California and Nevada for 30 years. Chris worked for a mining company, but then he decided to go it alone. Chris is genuinely interested in the area and its history – and he is certain that plenty of gold can still be found.

Chris is generous with his knowledge and he has a lot useful advice for other prospectors. He also gives tips on where to go looking for gold, and what is the best method of prospecting in that area. Chris thinks that joining a club is a good idea because you get to enjoy the company of others and learn from them at the same time. For Chris, it is not about making a huge amount of money. He says it is perfect for people who enjoy outdoor activities like hunting, hiking and fishing. But nothing, he says, can be compared with the excitement of finding your own piece of gold – however small!

There are two types of gold to be found. *Hard-rock* gold is when the gold is in its original location in the rock. *Placer* gold is when it has been broken free from the rock and moved some distance, often by a river. Because finding hard-rock gold usually requires expensive equipment, most amateurs look for small *nuggets* (single pieces of gold) or tiny *flakes* of placer gold. But if you do strike hard-rock gold, you are probably going to be very rich!

Using a metal detector is another common way of looking for gold. These can cost very little for a simple, used model. Better, more professional machines can cost thousands. As well as gold, of course, they help you find all metal objects, including coins.

4 Talk about one or more of the following questions with a partner.

- What do you think daily life was like for the forty-niners?
- Would you be interested in prospecting for gold? Why / Why not?

NATIONAL GEOGRAPHIC

6 Mysteries

> Grammar

Learn about modal verbs for speculation, and the second conditional.

> Vocabulary

Learn words connected with art, and for types of book.

Work with phrasal verbs, and noun + preposition combinations.

> Skills

Read about Agatha Christie, crop circles, and British best-sellers.

Listen to a story of an art forgery, and a radio programme about women authors.

Write an apology.

> Communicate

Make and respond to requests.

1 Put the words from the vocabulary box into two groups: *art* and *books*.

abstract	novel	portrait
drawing	oil	sculpture
fiction	painting	still life
landscape	play	watercolour
non-fiction	poetry	

2 Look at the photo on this page. What do you think it is? Use words from the vocabulary box.

3 6.1 Listen to three people talking about art. Which one is talking about the photo?

4 Do you like this kind of art? Tell your partner why or why not. What kind of art do you like?

6A A literary mystery

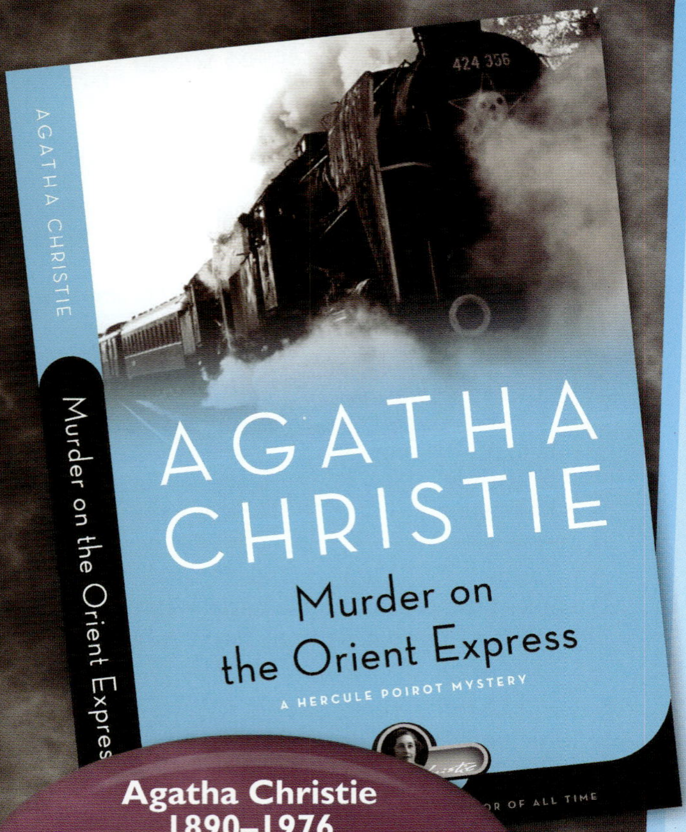

Agatha Christie
1890–1976
The 'Queen of Crime'
Novels, short stories and plays
The most translated author in the world
(more than 56 languages)
The best-selling writer of books
of all time

Tom: Oh, you're reading *Murder on the Orient Express*! I've read that – it's great! Have you worked out who the murderer is?

Chloe: No, and don't tell me! It's really confusing. All I know is, it can't be Poirot because he's the detective! So it must be one of the other passengers on the train – but at this point it could be anybody!

Tom: That's true. It might be the train driver …

Chloe: No, let's not talk about it. You'll give me too many clues.

Tom: OK. Did you know that Agatha Christie herself once disappeared? The police were looking for her all over the country.

Chloe: No way!

Tom: Yes, it was just before Christmas in 1926. She was missing for eleven days and then she turned up in a hotel in the north of England under a false name.

Chloe: So what had happened to her?

Tom: Well, a local doctor thought she could have lost her memory. On the other hand, she might have run away from her husband. They'd had a big argument because he wanted a divorce.

Chloe: But didn't she explain anything?

Tom: No, she never said a word. So because of that, some people decided that it must have been a fake disappearance – to get publicity for her books.

Chloe: Well, that couldn't have been true because she was already a best-selling author. Why would she need any more publicity? So what was the real explanation in the end?

Tom: Nobody knows. It's a real-life mystery.

Speaking

1 **Work in pairs. Tell your partner about two of these things.**

a book you're reading at the moment
a book you've read recently
your favourite book

2 **Put the types of book into two groups: *fiction* and *non-fiction*. How many authors or book titles can you name for each type of book?**

autobiography biography classic
cookery detective historical humour
mystery reference romance
science fiction thriller

Reading and listening

3 6.2 **Read and listen to the conversation. Are the sentences true or false – or is there not enough information to decide?**

1 Chloe thinks Poirot is a murderer.
2 Agatha Christie was married to a doctor.
3 Tom explains the plot of *Murder on the Orient Express*.
4 Agatha Christie wrote a mystery story about herself.

Working with words: phrasal verbs

4 Choose the correct meaning for these phrasal verbs from the conversation.

Have you worked out who the murderer is? = **a** decided, **b** asked

She turned up in a hotel. = **a** worked, **b** was found

She might have run away from her husband. = **a** left, **b** raced

See Working with words: Page 105

Grammar: modal verbs for speculation

5 Read the sentences (1–3) from the text and match them with the correct meaning (a–c).

1 It can't be Poirot.
2 It must be one of the other passengers.
3 It could be anybody.

a I think it's possible.
b I think it's impossible.
c I think it's almost certain.

See Grammar Explorer: Page 124

6 Look at this sentence and find three similar verbs in the text.

A local doctor thought she could have lost her memory.

7 Complete the table with the correct modal verbs.

Speculation about the present		
possible	may / might / (**1**)	*be*
impossible	(**2**)	
certain	(**3**)	
Speculation about the past		
possible	may / (**4**) .... / (**5**)	*have* + past participle
impossible	can't / (**6**)	
certain	(**7**)	

We don't normally use *can* to speculate.

8 Choose the correct options.

I love reading murder mystery stories. In my favourite murder mystery stories, there are often several suspects who (**1**) **might be** / **must be** the murderer. The first thing I do is write down the names of the people who are definitely innocent and (**2**) **have killed** / **couldn't have killed** the victim. As the story progresses and the evidence is revealed, sometimes I'm sure who the killer (**3**) **may be** / **must be**. Then I find he has an alibi and so (**4**) **couldn't have done** / **might have done** it. I don't like stories where it's too obvious who (**5**) **must have killed** / **can't have killed** the victim. I prefer books where you keep guessing right to the end.

9 Complete the sentences with the correct modal form of the verbs. Sometimes more than one answer is possible.

1 All the doors are locked. The killer .... (**escape**) through the window.
2 Hercule Poirot always catches the criminal. He .... (**be**) very intelligent.
3 The girl had the opportunity to steal the diamonds. It .... (**be**) her.
4 The main suspect was in prison at the time of the robbery. He .... (**do**) it.
5 We don't know where the attacker is. He .... (**be**) somewhere in the building.

Speaking

10 Work in pairs. Ask and answer questions about the picture. Use the verbs in the box or your own ideas. Then write sentences about the picture.

be come in eat go out hear leave open take out

A: *Why is the window open?*
B: *Someone must have come in that way.*
A: *Yes, or they might have gone out that way.*

11 Work in pairs. Imagine your English teacher hasn't come to class. Speculate on the reasons.

be sick sleep in have an accident forget be on a course win the lottery

Fast finishers

Find words on these pages for people who could appear in a murder mystery. The first letter is given: a – *attacker*, c, d, k, m, p, s, v.

6B Art mysteries

Crop circles alien art?

When crop circles first appeared in southern England, nobody knew how to explain them. What could be the cause of such unusual patterns in fields of crops? Many newspapers speculated that a strong wind might have flattened the plants. But if wind was the cause, the circles wouldn't be so complex. Some of the circles were like huge works of art. They had detailed, intricate patterns and were up to 200 metres across.

Other observers had a different reaction to the circles and said that they were too big and complex for humans to make. They decided that aliens must have made them! However, if extra-terrestrials wanted to make contact with humans, would they make crop circles? It seems like a bizarre explanation. Nevertheless, every summer more crop circles appeared and more tourists came to look at them. While some farmers were unhappy about the damage to their crops, others were unhappy that they didn't have a crop circle on their land. Many said, 'If I had one, I could earn money from the tourists.'

Eventually, two local painters, Doug Bower and Dave Chorley, explained how the hoax had begun. One summer evening in 1978, they were looking at an area of wind-flattened wheat. Bower said, 'If we made something like that, people would think a flying saucer had landed,' and that gave them the idea of trying to fool people.

Now there's a group of sculptors and artists from London called the 'Circlemakers'. And companies like Pepsi, Sky and the BBC pay to have their own circles made. However, the most curious thing about this hoax is that some people still believe crop circles are the work of aliens.

Reading and listening

1 Read the text quickly and answer the questions.

1. Where are crop circles found?
2. What are crop circles?
3. What do crop circles look like?

2 6.3 **Read and listen to the text. Find three explanations for the origin of crop circles. Which one is correct?**

Vocabulary: the art world

3 Complete the sentences with words from the box.

collector	expert	forgery	hoax
original	painter	sculptor	value

1. .... works of art by famous artists are unique.
2. Art often has a very high ....
3. A work of art can be bought by a museum or a private ....
4. A copy of an original work is called a fake or a ....
5. An art .... can sometimes be fooled by clever fakes.

Listening

4 6.4 **Listen to part of a radio programme about art mysteries. What happened? Choose the correct option (a–c).**

- **a** A forgery was sold to the Louvre Museum in Paris.
- **b** An original work of art was stolen from the Louvre Museum.
- **c** An expert from the Louvre bought a stolen work of art.

5 6.4 STUDY SKILLS **Listen to the story again. Make notes on what these people did. Compare with your partner.**

Eduardo de Valfierno | Vincenzo Peruggia | Yves Chaudron

6 **Valfierno was never caught by the police. Why do you think this was? Tell your partner.**

Working with words: noun + preposition

7 **Look at the examples. Then find these nouns in the text:** ***damage, area, idea, work.*** **Which prepositions follow these nouns?**

What could be the cause of such unusual patterns?
Other observers had a different reaction to the circles.

See Working with words: Page 105

Grammar: second conditional

8 **Complete these sentences from the text.**

Condition	Result
If wind was the cause,	the circles (**1**) .... be so complex.
If I had one,	I (**2**) .... earn money from the tourists.
If we made something like that,	people (**3**) .... think a flying saucer had landed.

We use *could* when the result is a possibility, but not a certainty.

We use *if* in the part of the sentence with the past simple verb. When the sentence starts with *if*, we use a comma at the end of the *if*-clause.

See Grammar Explorer: Page 124

9 **Choose the correct option.**

We use the second conditional to talk about **the past / the present and the future**.

10 **Match the sentence beginnings (1–5) with the endings (a–e). Then write the verbs in the correct forms.**

1. If our village .... (**have**) a crop circle,
2. If the forger .... (**be not**) such a good artist,
3. If you .... (**paint**) my portrait,
4. If a museum .... (**exhibit**) a fake,
5. If you .... (**say**) this was by da Vinci,

- **a** I .... (**put**) it on my wall.
- **b** nobody .... (**believe**) you.
- **c** people .... (**come**) to see it.
- **d** it .... (**be**) very embarrassing.
- **e** he .... (**not fool**) people.

Speaking

11 **Work in pairs. In how many ways can you complete the sentences?**

1. If aliens landed in the school yard, …
2. If I found a valuable painting, …
3. If I wanted to be a famous artist, …
4. If we appeared on TV, …
5. If I discovered a crop circle, …
6. If I sold one of my paintings for a lot of money, …

Study skills

Answering questions

When you listen to a text, you won't understand every word. Don't worry!

1. Focus on the questions you need to answer.
2. Listen for the answers and ignore the other information.
3. Don't be put off by unfamiliar words.

6C Requests

Reading and listening

1 6.5 **Read and listen to the dialogue. Which sign was in the entrance to the gallery?**

A

ADMISSION FREE
(EXCEPT FOR SPECIAL EXHIBITIONS)

B

NO PHOTOGRAPHY OR VIDEO FILMING
EXCEPT BY PERMISSION.

C

Please
DO NOT TAKE FOOD OR DRINK
INTO THE EXHIBITION ROOMS.

2 **Read the dialogue again. Answer the questions.**

1 What kind of art does Holly like?
2 What does Joe want to do?
3 What would Joe like to borrow?

Joe:	Thanks for coming with me, Holly. I know you don't really like and art stuff like that.
Holly:	That's not true. I like stuff that I understand, that's all.
Joe:	Can we start with the paintings and then look at the sculpture exhibition? Is that OK?
Holly:	Yes, sure.
Joe:	Oh, look at this!
Holly:	I don't really get abstract art. What is it supposed to be? A house?
Joe:	Maybe. Or it might be a human mind.
Holly:	If it was a human mind, it wouldn't have windows.
Joe:	Perhaps they're not windows!
Holly:	They look like windows to me.
Joe:	Well, I like it. It would be nice to get a photo of it. Do you mind holding my camera bag for a minute?
Holly:	No, not at all, but are you sure you can do that? Maybe you should ask the attendant.
Joe:	OK ... Excuse me, would it be all right if I took a photo of this picture?
Attendant:	I'm sorry, photography isn't allowed. There's a sign in the entrance.
Joe:	Oh, I didn't see it.
Attendant:	Would you like to buy a print? There are posters and postcards in the gallery shop.
Joe:	Right, thanks. So, Holly, is it all right if we go to the shop on the way out?
Holly:	Yes, that's fine.

An hour later

Joe:	Could you tell us the price of these posters, please?
Assistant:	Yes, of course. The cheapest ones start at £15.
Joe:	Oh! Holly, can you lend me some money? I'd really like to get a poster.
Holly:	Sorry, I've only got enough for my bus fare.
Joe:	OK, never mind. Could I have this postcard, please?
Assistant:	That's 95 pence. Thank you.

3 **Find the *Useful expressions* in the dialogue. Write the functions (1–3) in the gaps (a–c).**

1 asking someone to do something
2 responding to a request
3 making a request

USEFUL EXPRESSIONS

a ....
Can we start with the paintings?
Would it be all right if I took a photo?
Is it all right if we go to the shop?
Could I have this postcard, please?
b ....
Do you mind holding my camera bag?
Could you tell us the price of these posters, please?
Can you lend me some money?
c ....
Yes, sure.
No, not at all.
I'm sorry.
Yes, of course.

4 6.6 **Listen and repeat the *Useful expressions*. Focus on your intonation.**

5 **Where would you see these signs? Match the signs (A–C) with three of the places (1–4).**

1 an art gallery
2 a bookshop
3 a gift shop
4 a public library

6 **Work in pairs. For each situation, make a request, and respond. Take turns.**

1 You want to know if you can listen to your MP3 in the library.
2 You want a passer-by to take your photo.
3 You want to know if there is a café in the museum.
4 You want to borrow your friend's favourite book.

Pronunciation: words containing *au*

7 **How do you pronounce these words? Compare with your partner.**

astronaut audience audition aunt
Australia author autobiography
autograph because caught cause
daughter saucer sausage

8 6.7 **Listen and repeat the words in Exercise 7.**

Writing: an apology

1 **Read the note and the email. Find the following information.**

1 what happened
2 why it happened
3 the consequences

2 **Holly uses *due to* and *as a result* to explain the situation. Find these expressions in her message. Which expression introduces a cause? Which expression introduces a result?**

3 **Complete the sentences using *due to* or *as a result*.**

1 .... the terrible weather, the football match was cancelled.
2 The school bus broke down. ...., the day trip was cancelled.
3 .... the illness of the main singer, the school concert was postponed.
4 There was a fire in the school kitchen this morning. ...., there is no hot food today.

4 **Write an apology for one of the situations in Exercise 3. Give an explanation of the problem. Use Holly's message to help you.**

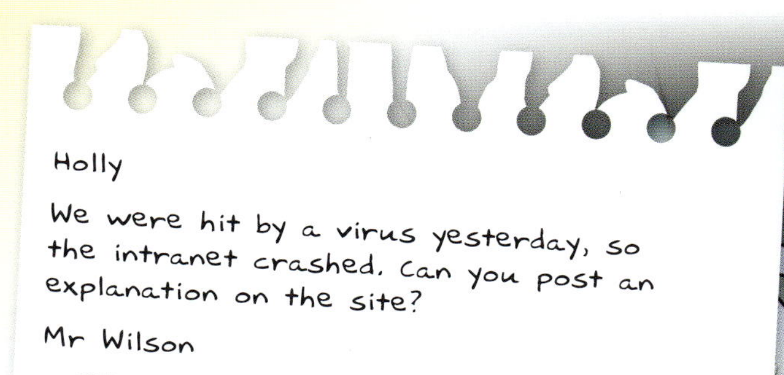
Holly

We were hit by a virus yesterday, so the intranet crashed. Can you post an explanation on the site?

Mr Wilson

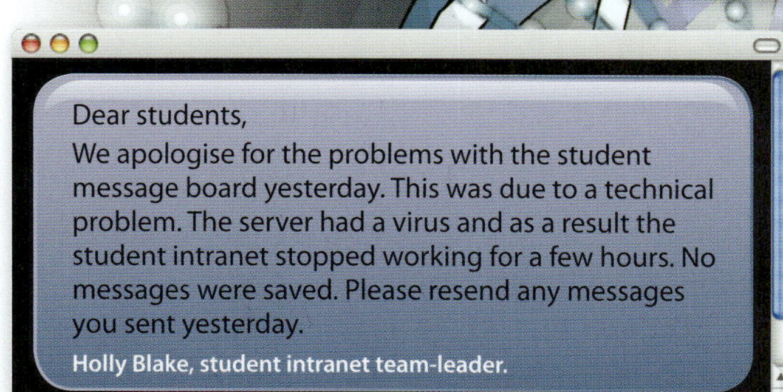
Dear students,
We apologise for the problems with the student message board yesterday. This was due to a technical problem. The server had a virus and as a result the student intranet stopped working for a few hours. No messages were saved. Please resend any messages you sent yesterday.
Holly Blake, student intranet team-leader.

6D British best-sellers

Culture

Reading

1 **Work in pairs. Do you agree with any of the sentences?**

1. I like books that scare me.
2. I like to escape into a different world when I read.
3. I like stories that keep me awake at night.
4. I like to read about characters that have magic adventures.

2 6.8 **Read about some books by British authors and write the name of the books.**

1. .... is about a struggle between good and evil.
2. .... was originally written as a children's story.
3. .... is about a frightening experiment.

3 **Read the text again. Which sentences (1–4) in Exercise 1 are about Gothic horror and which are about fantasy literature?**

4 **Find two more words or expressions in the text with similar meanings to each of these words.**

book **genre** **best-seller**

5 **Read the first sentence. Complete the second sentence so that it gives the same information.**

1 a It was such a successful novel that other writers copied it.
  b The novel was .... that other writers copied it.

2 a A studio made the book into a film.
  b The book .... into a film.

3 a Wizards became popular as a result of *Harry Potter's* success.
  b .... *Harry Potter's* success, wizards became popular.

'Best-sellers' are not simply a modern-day publishing phenomenon. There have always been books that were instantly popular.

Occasionally, a novel is so successful that it starts a new kind of writing. *Frankenstein*, published in 1818 by Mary Shelley, is a good example. The scary story of Victor Frankenstein, a scientist who manages to create a human life, was an immediate success with the public. It was the first real Gothic horror novel. The book was quickly adapted for the theatre and as a result became even more well-known. Nowadays, we are all familiar with Hollywood versions of a 'mad scientist' who is forced to destroy his evil creation.

An evil force is also at the centre of *The Strange Case of Dr Jekyll and Mr Hyde* (1886) by Robert Louis Stevenson. The story of a 'good' man who regularly turns into an evil version of himself appealed to many readers. The book was a best-seller within months. It was the origin of 20th-century characters like the Hulk and 'superheroes' who lead a double life.

Gothic horror was, in fact, one of the key literary genres of 19th-century Britain. Perhaps the best-selling genre of the 20th century was fantasy, characterised by parallel worlds inhabited by magic creatures. J.R.R.Tolkien is often called the 'father of modern fantasy' literature. Although he didn't originate the style, it became very popular due to the success of *The Hobbit* and *The Lord of the Rings* series. Tolkien had written *The Hobbit* for children and he was surprised when it was a hit with adults too. Another best-selling fantasy series, the *Harry Potter* books, by J.K. Rowling, also appeals to both children and adults. How many people do you know who have read these books?

Listening

6 6.9 **Which of these writers are women? Listen to a radio programme and check.**

J.K. Rowling   C.S. Lewis   J.R.R.Tolkien
George Eliot   Acton Bell

7 6.9 **Listen again and choose the correct option (a–c).**

1 What happened when some journalists found out that Mary Shelley was the author of *Frankenstein?*
  - **a** They refused to review the book.
  - **b** They refused to believe she'd written it.
  - **c** They gave it a bad review.

2 Why did Mary Ann Evans use a man's name?
  - **a** So that she could earn more money.
  - **b** So that she would be considered as a serious author.
  - **c** So that she could write more than one style of novel.

3 Why did J.K. Rowling's publisher want her to use her initials?
  - **a** Because they thought boys might not read books by a woman.
  - **b** Because her first names are very complicated.
  - **c** Because they didn't know whether she was a woman or a man.

Art and English

Leonardo da Vinci

1 Write down three things you know about Leonardo da Vinci.
Read the text and see if these things are mentioned.

Self-portrait, 1515

Leonardo da Vinci was born in Florence, Italy, in 1452. At that time, Europe was at the start of a long period of artistic and intellectual development called the Renaissance. Da Vinci was a perfect example of a 'Renaissance man'. He was incredibly talented in many areas of both the arts and the sciences, and today is regarded as one of the greatest painters of all time. He also did thousands of drawings, not only artistic but also technical. As he himself wrote, in 1482: 'I can execute sculpture in bronze, marble or clay. Also, in painting, I can do as much as anyone, whoever he may be.'

Da Vinci had many ideas that seem modern even today. He was a vegetarian and in his painting 'The Last Supper' he didn't show any meat on the table. He was obsessed with birds and flight. He used to buy birds in cages and release them into the wild. His writings showed that he understood some laws of physics 200 years before Sir Isaac Newton. Many of his notes and drawings have survived – 13,000 pages of them – ranging from shopping lists to plans for helicopters! Some of his most important scientific writings are now owned by Bill Gates. Da Vinci wrote his notes in code and in right-to-left mirror writing. Perhaps this was because he didn't want people to steal his ideas, or perhaps, since he was left-handed, it was easier. We will probably never know.

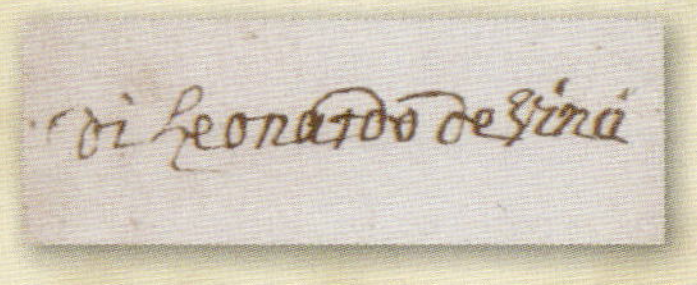

2 Read the text again. Find all other things you find out about da Vinci.

3 What do you think is the most interesting thing about da Vinci? Compare with your partner.

Project

Choose a popular novel from your country. Write a paragraph about it and use illustrations of the story.

Consolidation Units 5 and 6

Listening

Identifying the main idea

- Read the task instruction and the options. Identify the overall topic if it is mentioned.
- Look carefully at the meaning of each option – remember the topic words may be similar in each case.
- The first time you listen, choose the correct answer. The second time, check your answers.

1 Look at the three options in a listening task. Which topic have they got in common?

The man talks about

a reading for pleasure.
b the books he reads on holiday.
c his favourite author.

2 Match the groups of words (1–3) with the options (a–c) in Exercise 1.

1 guidebooks beach airport bookshop
2 detective stories interesting magazines hobby
3 writer first book new title

3 6.10 **Now listen and tick the words you hear in Exercise 2.**

4 6.10 **Listen again and do the task in Exercise 1.**

5 6.11 **You will hear someone talking about her hobby. Listen and choose the correct option (a–c).**

a The woman is a sculptor.
b The woman makes presents out of unusual objects.
c The woman does abstract paintings.

Reading

Identifying the situation

- Find the key words in the notices which can help you identify the place or situation.
- Read the first notice again, look at the options and find the one which matches.
- Repeat this for the other notices. Then check them again.

1 Read the notices from an art gallery. Find the words which tell you the notice is from an art gallery.

1
Watercolour exhibition
25 Feb – 24 March.
Free entry.

2
BRITISH SCULPTURE IN THE 20TH CENTURY →

2 Read these notices and choose the key words.

A
No outdoor shoes allowed in the gym.

B
Please switch off mobiles. No loud conversations.

C
History of science interactive display, downstairs.

D
Special offer! Half price off selected titles in mysteries and thrillers!

3 Write places where you can see the notices in Exercise 2.

4 Match the signs (a–d) in Exercise 2 with the places (1–5). There is one extra place.

1 in a museum
2 in a school
3 in a bookshop
4 in a cinema
5 in a library

a/an or *the*?

We use *a/an* to talk about one of many things, not a specific thing. We use *the* to refer to a specific thing.

Leonardo da Vinci was a genius. He had an idea for a helicopter.

Have you been to the new Leonardo da Vinci exhibition yet?

1 Complete the sentences with *a, an* or *the*.

1 Have you ever seen .... vampire?
2 I'm going to write .... novel.
3 Which was .... first book Agatha Christie wrote?
4 I got .... amazing picture for my birthday.

the for specific things

We use *the* with things we have already mentioned and when the context makes it clear which thing we mean.

I'm wearing a gold ring and a silver ring. The silver ring is new.

I love this painting. The colours are bright and exciting.

2 Complete the sentences with *a, an* or *the*.

1 I like my English class. .... teacher is great.
2 We've got .... cat and .... dog. .... cat is called Ginger.
3 We're going to .... cinema. Do you want to come?
4 I do my homework after school. I do it in .... living room.

the only one

We use *the* when there's only one of the thing we're talking about.

3 Choose the correct option.

1 I like looking at **a** / **the** moon.
2 We live in **a** / **the** big city.
3 Pollution is bad for **an** / **the** environment.
4 Are you connected to **a** / **the** Internet?
5 Which is **a** / **the** oldest World Wonder?

the with types of things and groups

We use *the* + noun or plural nouns without *the* to talk about types of things.

The kangaroo is an Australian animal.
Koalas live in trees.

4 Choose the correct option.

1 **Bats** / **The bat** is nocturnal.
2 **Helicopters** / **The helicopter** was first drawn by Leonardo da Vinci.
3 **Violins** / **The violin** are string instruments.
4 **Kiwis** / **The kiwi** is found only in New Zealand.
5 **Crocodiles** / **The crocodile** live in rivers.

We use *the* + adjective to talk about a group of people.

5 Complete the sentences with phrases from the box. There are two extra phrases.

the homeless	the military	the poor
the rich	the sick	the young

1 Older people don't understand .... these days.
2 It's a luxury hotel especially for ....
3 I'd like to be a doctor and help ....
4 We need to build more houses for ....

Names

We use *the* with the names of seas, oceans, rivers, canals, deserts, groups of islands, mountain ranges, countries ending in *-s* and *Kingdom* or *Republic*

6 Read the sentences. Cross out *the* where it is not needed.

1 We're going on holiday to the United States and the Mexico.
2 I live in the United Kingdom, which is part of the Europe.
3 The Irish Sea is between the Ireland and the England.
4 I'd love to go climbing in the Alps or swimming in the Bahamas.
5 The Sahara and the Nile are in the Africa.

Review Units 5 and 6

Vocabulary

1 Write the materials.

1 ....
2 ....
3 ....
4 ....
5 ....

1 mark per item: .../5 marks

2 Write the shapes.

1 ....
2 ....
3 ....
4 ....
5 ....

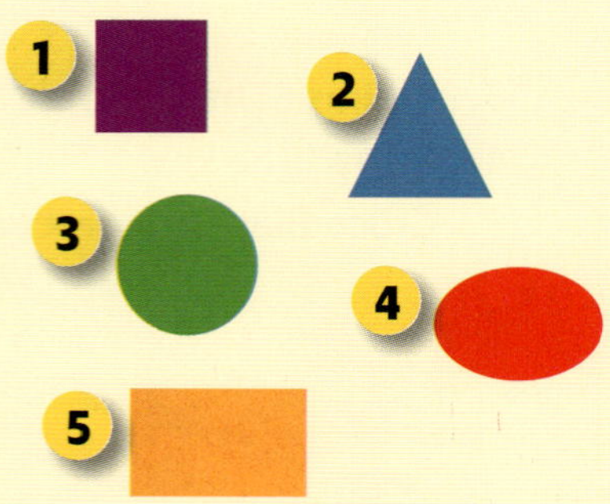

1 mark per item: .../5 marks

3 Write the type of book.

1 about somebody's own life ....
2 about a love story ....
3 about food and recipes ....
4 about the past ....
5 it makes you laugh ....

1 mark per item: .../5 marks

4 Write the words.

1 a painting of a person ....
2 a painting of the country ....
3 it's performed in a theatre ....
4 a picture done with a pencil ....
5 a painting of objects ....

1 mark per item: .../5 marks

5 Write the prepositions.

1 What's your reaction .... this sculpture?
2 Do you believe .... ghosts?
3 We think our dog has run ....
4 What was the cause .... the accident?
5 My pen has run .... of ink.

1 mark per item: .../5 marks

Grammar

6 Complete the sentences with the correct form of the passive.

1 Petra (**build**) .... 2,000 years ago.
2 This statue (**restore**) .... now.
3 The tomb (**visit**) .... by many people since its discovery.
4 The ship disappeared in the Atlantic. It (**not / find**) ....
5 You can't visit the church while it (**clean**) ....

1 mark per item: .../5 marks

7 Rewrite each active sentence in the passive.

1 Fire did not destroy the statue.
2 How did they move the rock?
3 Why have they closed the building?
4 Nobody has revealed the secret.
5 When did they abandon the city?

1 mark per item: .../5 marks

8 Choose the correct option.

1 The museum **can** / **will** be opened by the Queen.
2 Most stars **can't** / **will** be seen without a telescope.
3 Many objects **can** / **must** be made from gold.
4 Phones **must** / **won't** be switched off at all times.
5 The work **mustn't** / **won't** be finished in time.

1 mark per item: .../5 marks

9 Choose the correct option.

The door was locked, so the thief (**1**) **can** / **must** have used a key. He (**2**) **can't** / **might** have gone into the house when the owners left. They could smell cigarettes, so the thief (**3**) **must** / **mustn't** smoke. He (**4**) **can** / **can't** be very clever because he didn't steal valuable objects. Or he (**5**) **could** / **mustn't** have been interrupted when the owners returned.

1 mark per item: .../5 marks

10 Complete the second conditional sentences.

1 I'd collect art if I (**be**) .... rich.
2 If you saw a UFO, (**you / believe**) .... it?
3 If I had a garden, I (**grow**) .... vegetables.
4 I (**be**) .... happy if I (**pass**) .... the exam.
5 If the shop was open, we (**can / go**) .... in.

1 mark per item: .../5 marks

Communicate

11 Match the sentence beginnings (1–5) with the endings (a–e).

1 Could you
2 Yes,
3 Would it be all right if we
4 No,
5 Do you mind

a not at all.
b showing me this picture, please?
c of course.
d sat here?
e tell me the time, please?

2 marks per item: …/10 marks

12 Complete the dialogue with the expressions.

because so that what for why to get my hair cut

Kate: Can you give me ten pounds, please?
Dad: (**1**) ………… ? That's a lot of money.
Kate: I want (**2**) ………… .
Dad: (**3**) ………… do you want to do that? It looks lovely the way it is.
Kate: (**4**) ………… it's too long, Dad.
Dad: OK then, here you are.
Kate: Thanks. The hairdresser's is on Percy Street.
Dad: Why are you telling me that?
Kate: (**5**) ………… you can come and get me later!

2 marks per item: …/10 marks

13 Does the 'o' in these words sound like the *o* in *gold* /əʊ/ or *some* /ʌ/? Write G or S.

1 above …………
2 chose …………
3 come …………
4 done …………
5 money …………
6 old …………
7 oval …………
8 so …………
9 stone …………
10 won …………

1 mark per item: …/10 marks

14 Complete the sentences with these words.

as as a result due to so that to

1 The road was closed ………… the snow.
2 ………… the weather was so bad, we stayed at home.
3 I used my mobile ………… call for help.
4 It snowed all night. ………… , there was no electricity.
5 We lit some candles ………… we could see.

2 marks per item: …/10 marks

15 Complete the letter with these words.

a all any at for if of some the to

Dear Parents,

We apologise (**1**) ………… the changes to our parent–teacher meetings this term. This is because (**2**) ………… the building work in (**3**) ………… school. As you know, we are having (**4**) ………… fire alarm system installed, following the damage (**5**) ………… the gym last month. Since this work will affect (**6**) ………… the classrooms, there are changes to (**7**) ………… meeting dates and places. Please look (**8**) ………… the new programme and contact Mr Banks (**9**) ………… you have (**10**) ………… questions.

Mrs Smith
Head teacher

1 mark per item: …/10 marks

Total: …/100

I can…

I can talk about purpose and reason.
I can make and respond to requests.

PROJECT A great artist

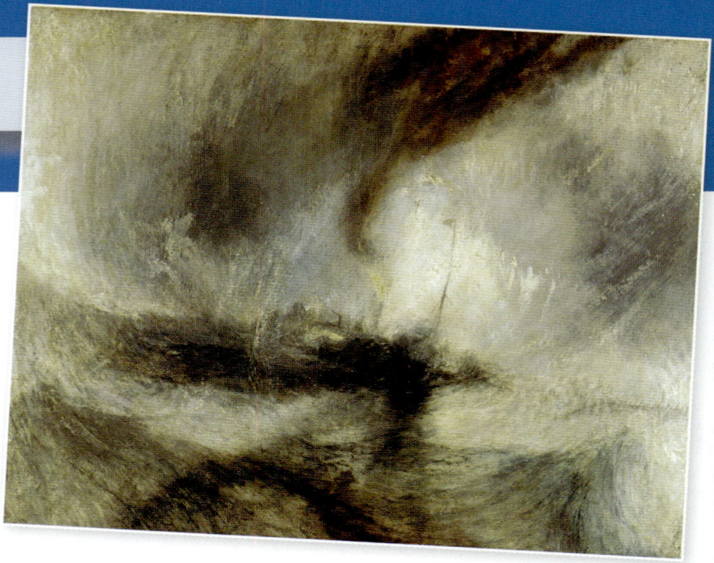

1 **Look at the picture and say what you think about it. Use some of the following phrases:**

It could/must/can't be ...   It could/must/can't have ...
The painter could/must/can't have ...
The weather could/must/can't have ...

2 **Read the article and answer the questions.**

Joseph Mallord William Turner was born in London in 1775. He studied art from a very young age and at 13 he was selling his own drawings from his father's shop window. When he was just 15, one of his paintings was put in an exhibition at the Royal Academy. Slowly, he became well known and he became a member of the Royal Academy. Although he was better known for his oil paintings, he also made prints and he was recognised as a master of watercolours too.

1 Which statement is true about the young Turner?
- **a** He made money from his art.
- **b** He worked for his father.
- **c** He started studying art at the age of 13.

2 Turner ...
- **a** preferred watercolours to printmaking.
- **b** was much better at oil painting.
- **c** was very good at more than one type of painting.

Turner travelled throughout Europe and he particularly loved Venice. He was interested in light and he was passionate about the weather and the changes he noted on the sea and in the sky. As time went on, the objects in his paintings became less clear and the paintings became a romantic expression of his own feelings. His work was admired by many other painters such as Claude Monet, who was keen to study his style.

3 The weather was important to Turner because
- **a** it often stopped him from painting.
- **b** he liked the effect that it had on the light.
- **c** he disliked the English weather so he travelled in Europe.

4 As time passed, Turner
- **a** painted less detail in his work.
- **b** studied the styles of others.
- **c** was less sure of what to paint.

Turner spent a great deal of his adult life alone. He even travelled alone, and he never let anyone see him while he was working. No one knows the cause of his unsociable behaviour. He might have been worried that people would copy his technique, but it is more likely that he had become so involved in his work that he found it difficult to be with people.

5 The writer says that Turner
- **a** was worried about people stealing his paintings.
- **b** sometimes worked with other painters.
- **c** did not like to be with other people.

Turner died in 1851. He had wanted all of his paintings to stay in one building for the people of Britain but this didn't happen until many years after his death. In more recent years, a new wing of the Tate Gallery in London was opened to display Turner's paintings. The Turner Prize, which has been a famous art prize in Britain since 1984, was named after him.

6 We can understand from the article that Turner must have ...
- **a** found a building for all of his paintings.
- **b** expressed a wish for his paintings to stay together.
- **c** been quickly forgotten after his death.

Project

Write an article about a famous artist from your country.
- Say what kind of art he/she is famous for
- Give brief biographical information.
- Mention why he/she is different to other artists
- Include any interesting facts you can find about the artist's life or work
- Remember to use modal verbs for speculation
- Find pictures to show the artist's work

Original works by Turner have a very high value. In 2010, his painting *Modern Rome – Campo Vaccino* was sold for a record-breaking price of nearly 30 million pounds.

Moments in history

7

> Grammar

Learn about the third conditional, *could/should have done* and *wish* and *if only*.

> Vocabulary

Learn words for science and technology, and words connected with politics.Work with prefixes, and suffixes.

> Skills

Read about mathematical and scientific codes, Nelson Mandela, and South African life.

Listen to comments about four famous people, and a tour of Cape Town.

Write a story.

> Communicate

Talk about regrets and make criticisms.

1 Look at the photo and choose the best options to complete the description.

This scientist is doing an (**1**) **experiment** / **innovation** in a (**2**) **data** / **laboratory**. He's probably testing a (**3**) **theory** / **knowledge** as part of his (**4**) **research** / **discovery**. The (**5**) **results** / **machine** could lead to a new medical application.

2 Work in pairs. What are these scientists famous for?

Marie Curie	Charles Darwin
Alexander Fleming	Guglielmo Marconi
Isaac Newton	Louis Pasteur

3 7.1 **Listen to the conversation and check your answers to Exercise 2.**

4 Work in pairs. Who was the greatest scientist of all time? Explain your reasons to your partner. Use the words in the vocabulary box to help you.

application	innovation	research
data	knowledge	result
discovery	laboratory	test
experiment	machine	theory

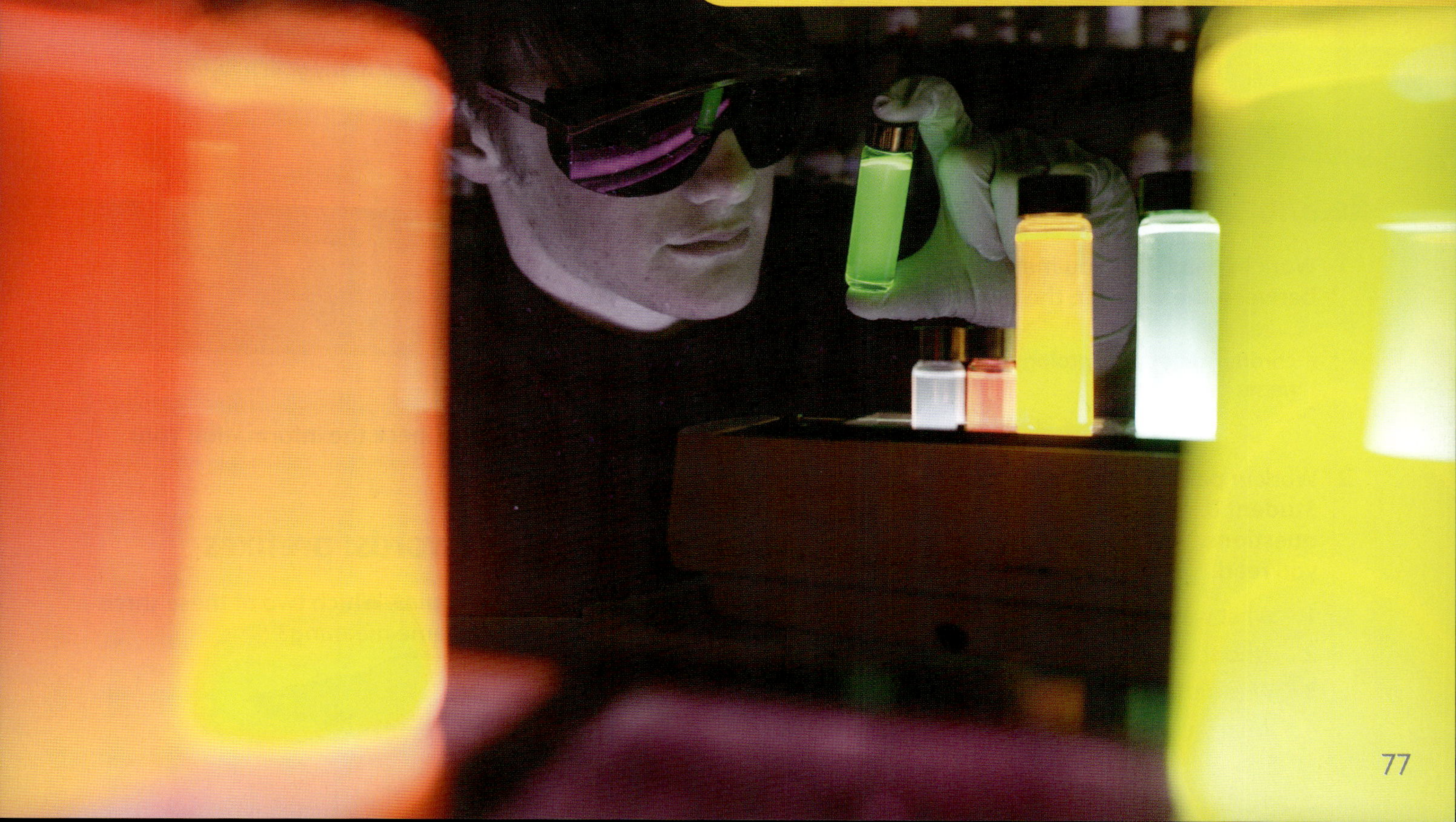

7A Cracking the code

THE ENIGMA STORY

In 1932, Marian Rejewski was working at the Polish cypher bureau. At that time, the German military used a machine, called Enigma I, to encrypt messages. No one could decipher them until Rejewski cracked the code. Now Poland was able to decode secret German military plans. A few weeks before World War II broke out, Poland shared this knowledge with France and Great Britain. Machines that could crack the Enigma code helped to save many lives and they contributed to many military victories. In 1944, they were important in the battle to free Europe. But if Rejewski hadn't cracked the code, the course of the war would have been very different.

THE DNA STORY

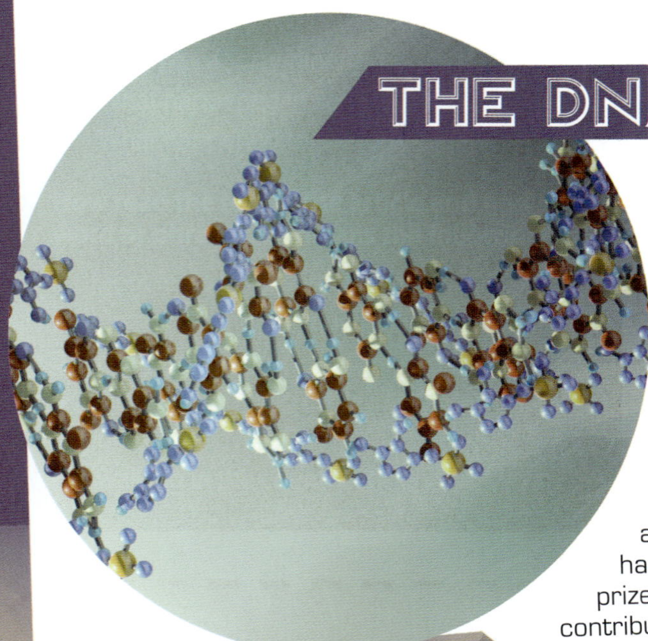

In the early 1950s, Rosalind Franklin was doing research at Kings College, London. She'd got her PhD in physical chemistry from Cambridge University several years earlier. As part of her research, Franklin developed a technique for taking X-rays of DNA. Her work was essential to two biologists at Kings College, James Crick and Francis Watson. They were trying to work out the structure of DNA. They published their theory in 1953. They wouldn't have been successful if Franklin hadn't shown them her X-rays. In 1962, Crick and Watson, with another scientist, Maurice Wilkins, were awarded the Nobel Prize for their work. Franklin, sadly, had died aged 37 in 1958. Would she have shared the prize with them if she'd still been alive? Possibly not, since her contribution was not acknowledged until many years later.

Reading

1 **Work in pairs. Can you make connections between the words in the box?**

> chromosome cryptology cipher DNA gene message

2 **Work in pairs. Student A, read *The Enigma Story*. Student B, read *The DNA Story*. Answer the questions. Then tell your partner about the story you read.**

1. What was the 'code'?
2. Who shared information?
3. Who did they share it with?
4. What were the consequences?

3 **Read the stories. Check the information your partner gave you.**

Working with words: prefixes

4 **Look at the examples. Which two of these three words have the same meaning?**

encrypt decipher decode

See Working with words: Page 106

Grammar: third conditional

5 Complete these sentences from the text.

1. If Rejewski hadn't cracked the code, the course of the war .... very different.
2. They wouldn't have been successful if Franklin .... them her X-rays.
3. .... she .... the prize with them if she'd still been alive?

See Grammar Explorer: Page 124

6 Read the sentences in Exercise 5 again and choose the correct option.

1. Poland **shared** / **did not share** information.
2. Franklin **shared** / **did not share** her data.
3. Franklin **was** / **was not** alive when the Nobel prize was awarded.

We use the third conditional to talk about imagined results of events in the past.

7 Mark the correct position of *if* in each sentence.

e.g. The course of the war would have been different ..*if*.. Poland hadn't shared the Enigma information.

1. Rejewski hadn't worked at the Polish cypher bureau, he wouldn't have deciphered the code.
2. Would Germany have used the Enigma machines they had known the Polish could decode their messages?
3. Franklin wouldn't have studied chemistry her father hadn't allowed it.
4. Franklin had gone to a different university, Watson and Crick wouldn't have met her.

8 Complete the sentences with the correct form of the verbs.

1. If Roentgen .... (**not discover**) X-rays, Franklin .... (**not be able**) to do her research.
2. .... Newton .... (**write**) the laws of motion if he .... (**not study**) physics?
3. If Leonardo da Vinci .... (**be**) right-handed, ... he .... (**write**) in code?
4. If Einstein .... (**obey**) his father, he .... (**become**) an electrical engineer.
5. Marconi .... (**not develop**) the radio so quickly if he .... (**stay**) in Italy.

9 Read about the discovery of penicillin. Then write four sentences in the third conditional. Use the two underlined verbs in each sentence. Use *not* where necessary.

Alexander Fleming (**1**) went on holiday and (**1**) left some dishes in his laboratory. He hadn't (**2**) cleaned the dishes, so bacteria (**2**) grew on them. When he got back from holiday, he didn't (**3**) throw the dishes away, and he (**3**) noticed one unusual dish where the bacteria hadn't grown.

Fleming saw a mould on the dish, and realised that this mould was killing the bacteria. He (**4**) investigated the mould and (**4**) discovered penicillin.

10 Imagine you are the person in each situation. What would you say? Write four sentences using the third conditional.

1 study / understand

2 not explode / listen to the teacher

3 not get lost / bring a map

4 follow the recipe / not be a disaster

Speaking

11 Work in pairs. Tell your partner about a time something went wrong for you or your family. Use the ideas in the box or your own ideas.

family pets on holiday cooking going out domestic disasters family parties

A: *Once, our dog ran away. If the door had been closed, he wouldn't have got out.*

B: *Did you find him?*

Fast finishers

Look at this sentence beginning. How many endings can you think of?
If I'd worked harder, …

7B Rebels

In one way, the fact that Nelson Mandela became president of his country is not a surprise – his great-grandfather was king of the Thembu people in South Africa. On the other hand, Mandela spent 27 years of his life in a South African prison as a political prisoner!

Mandela was born in 1918. As a child, he did well at school and went on to university. (**1**) ....

The big change in Mandela's life came in 1948. The National Party was elected and it introduced a policy of apartheid. Mandela joined the ANC (African National Congress) campaign of non-violent protest against apartheid. By this time, he had qualified as a lawyer and was influenced by the ideas of Mahatma Gandhi, also a lawyer.

If the peaceful campaign had achieved progress in South Africa, the ANC would not have changed their tactics. In 1961, the ANC started bombing government offices, although they avoided injuring people. (**2**) .... In 1963, Mandela was sent to prison for life. He was allowed one visitor and one letter every six months. The world should have forgotten him, but instead he became the focus of an international movement against South African policies.

Mandela could have left prison in 1985, but he refused to accept the conditions that the government set. (**3**) .... Eventually, President F.W. de Klerk gave Mandela his freedom on 11 February 1990. Four years later, he won South Africa's first multi-racial elections and became president.

Nelson Mandela

Speaking

1 **Look at the photos. What do you know about these people? Tell your partner.**

Reading and listening

2 **Work in pairs. How do you say these words in your language? For each word, write N (noun) or V (verb). Some words are both.**

> campaign democracy election freedom
> government law leader policy
> politics protest right vote

3 STUDY SKILLS **Read quickly through the text about Nelson Mandela. How many words from the vocabulary box can you find?**

4 7.2 **Read and listen to the text. Are the sentences true or false – or is there not enough information to decide?**

1. Mandela's family was important in South African society.
2. Mandela was the leader of the National Party.
3. Nobody outside South Africa knew about Mandela until 1990.
4. F.W. de Klerk was against apartheid.

Grammar: *could/should have done*

5 **Look at the examples (1–2). Match them with the meanings (a–b).**

1. The world should have forgotten him.
2. Mandela could have left prison in 1985.

a. It was possible, but it did not happen.
b. It was logical, but it did not happen.

See Grammar Explorer: Page 125

6 **Read the text again and complete the gaps (1–3) with the sentences (a–d). There is one extra sentence.**

a. He could have spent his whole life in prison, but a new president was elected.
b. He should have graduated, but he had to leave after protesting against the university policies.
c. He could have met Mahatma Gandhi when he was in prison.
d. However, many people thought the ANC shouldn't have taken this action.

Emmeline Pankhurst

Mahatma Gandhi

Che Guevara

Aung San Suu Kyi

7 Read the first sentence. Complete the second sentence with *could, couldn't, should* or *shouldn't*.

e.g. I didn't know you were looking for a dictionary. I could have lent you mine.

1 I worked hard for that exam. I .... have got a better mark.

2 I think you were the best in the competition. You .... have won.

3 Why didn't you tell me you were in hospital? I .... have visited you.

4 You did your best. You .... have done any more.

5 I made a mistake. I voted for Shaw, but I .... have voted for Rogers.

6 The result of the election was a surprise. Nobody .... have predicted it.

Listening

8 7.3 **Listen to four people talking about the people in the photos on this page. Match the speakers (1–4) with the statements (a–e). There is one extra statement.**

a Without this person's actions, British women wouldn't have won the right to vote. ....

b This person's political party should have been in government after the election. ....

c This person could have had a comfortable life as a doctor. ....

d The American civil rights movement couldn't have existed without this person. ....

e Without this person's influence, many more people could have died in India. ....

9 7.3 **Listen again and complete the sentences.**

1 Mahatma Gandhi lived in .... and India.

2 Aung San Suu Kyi was a .... in her own home.

3 Emmeline Pankhurst and her .... went to prison several times.

4 Che Guevara worked as a .... with the poor and the sick.

Working with words: suffixes

10 Look at the examples. Find other words in Exercise 2 which can have different forms.

politics: He was a political prisoner.

election: The National Party was elected.

See Working with words: Page 106

Speaking

11 Work in groups and discuss these questions.

1 Who or what did the people on this page rebel against?

2 What would you have done in these situations?

3 Can you name any more rebels?

Study skills

Dictionary skills

1 Your dictionary sometimes gives more than one meaning for a word. Look carefully at the context to make sure you choose the right meaning.

2 How many meanings can you find for these words: *right* and *course*?

3 What's the difference between these words: *politics*, *policy* and *police*?

7C Regrets and criticisms

Reading and listening

1 7.4 **Read and listen to the dialogue. Answer the questions.**

1 Who hasn't done the project?
2 Who are Dan, Holly and Joe waiting for?
3 Who comes to the class?

2 **Joe mentions two problems he had with his project. What are they? What is Dan's comment in each case?**

3 **Find the *Useful expressions* in the dialogue. Which expressions show regret? Which ones show criticism?**

USEFUL EXPRESSIONS

I wish I was more organised.
You should have asked Mrs Evans for more time.
I wish I'd spoken to her last week.
I wish we could help you.
I shouldn't have chosen this topic.

See Grammar Explorer: Page 125

Dan: Oh, I'm so tired! I was up until one o'clock this morning, printing out my project. I wish I was more organised.

Holly: It looks great! Here's mine. I did it last week. I hate leaving things until the last minute. What about you, Joe?

Joe: I haven't finished mine. I didn't have enough time.

Holly: What? But it's worth about 30 per cent of your mark!

Dan: You should have asked Mrs Evans for more time.

Joe: I know. I wish I'd spoken to her last week. It's too late now.

Holly: Oh, Joe! I wish we could help you.

Joe: Thanks, but it's my own fault. I shouldn't have chosen this topic. It's really difficult.

Dan: Well, if you'd told us earlier, we could have helped you with it.

Holly: Here comes Mrs Evans. Let's go in.

Dan: No, it isn't Mrs Evans – it's Mr Lee! That's weird.

Mr Lee: Good morning, everyone. Now, Mrs Evans is ill, but she'll be back next Monday. She says you should carry on with your projects and you can hand them in next week.

Dan: Joe Todd, you are so lucky!

4 7.5 **Listen and repeat the *Useful expressions*. Focus on your intonation.**

5 7.6 **Listen to each statement and choose the best response (a–c).**

1 a You shouldn't have gone to bed so late.
 b You should have stayed up.
 c I wish I hadn't gone to bed early.

2 a You shouldn't have set your alarm clock.
 b I should have been at school.
 c I wish I'd set my alarm clock.

3 a I wish I'd taken your photo.
 b You should have read the instructions.
 c You shouldn't have used my camera.

4 a I should have told you yesterday.
 b I wish we'd gone camping.
 c I wish you'd told me earlier.

Speaking

6 **Work in pairs. For each situation, make one comment of regret and one of criticism. Take turns.**

A: *I wish I hadn't eaten all of that!*

B: *You should have shared it with me!*

1 eat / share

2 study / help

3 practise / bring

4 wear / borrow

Pronunciation: silent letters

7 7.7 **Listen to these words and look at the spelling. Find the silent letters in each word. Then listen, check and repeat.**

campaign castle doubt foreign half island knowledge psychologist scientist would

Writing: a story

1 **Read Fay's story and answer the questions.**

1 When did the events in the story happen?
2 Who and what was involved?
3 What two things did Fay do to solve the problem?
4 How did the story end?

2 **Look at the words in red. What kind of words are they? What follows them?**

3 **Rewrite the pairs of sentences as one sentence. Use the preposition given.**

1 I switched on my computer. Then I checked my emails. (**after**)
2 I wrote down my password. Then I logged off the site. (**before**)
3 I solved the problem. I didn't phone the helpline. (**without**)
4 I changed my password. I made my account more secure. (**by**)

4 **Think about a time you had a problem. Write a paragraph about what happened and how you solved the problem. Use Fay's story to help you.**

My IT disaster story

Last week I had an IT disaster! I forgot my email password! I should have written it down somewhere when I set up the account, but I didn't. After trying about six different versions of my password, my email account locked me out. I had no idea how to unlock it and I was desperate to read my emails. There was a telephone helpline number, but they are usually really expensive. I decided to ask my friend Dan before phoning the helpline. But after spending about half an hour on it, he gave up! So I rang the helpline and the first thing the girl said was 'Press the CAPS LOCK key.' It worked!

7D South African life

Reading

1 **Work in pairs. Imagine you went on holiday to South Africa. What languages would you hear around you? What animals would you see?**

2 **Read the text quickly and check your answers to Exercise 1.**

Culture

Rainbow Nation

In the northern part of South Africa, archaeologists have discovered some particularly interesting human fossils. They are more than two million years old – the earliest ever found. The region is known as the 'Cradle of Humankind'. Today, South Africans come from places as different as India and the Netherlands as well as southern Africa itself. Each group has its own history and language. There are eleven official languages, including English, Afrikaans and IsiZulu, and many more unofficial ones. This exceptionally colourful mix of cultures gives South Africa its unofficial name, Rainbow Nation.

Sea life

On South Africa's east coast, the warm Indian Ocean comes down from the tropics. To the west, the cold Atlantic currents arrive from the Antarctic. It's a recipe for a rich diversity of sea life and about 2,000 species visit these waters at different times of the year. It's one of the best places in the world to see whales close up. The blue whale is incredibly large. At 30 metres long and 170 tons, it's the biggest animal in the world. The humpback is slightly smaller but gives spectacular displays, throwing its body out of the water. Humpbacks often come surprisingly close to boats to have a look at the human species!

On safari

South Africa covers one per cent of the land surface of Earth, yet it has amazingly varied habitats. Ten per cent of the planet's bird, fish and plant species, and six per cent of mammal and reptile species, live here. From antelopes to zebras, the country is bursting with wildlife. The Kruger National Park is home to rhinoceros, leopards, elephants and the symbolic springbok, whose name is given to the national rugby team. Both local people and foreign tourists enjoy thrilling safari holidays here.

3 7.8 **Read the text again and answer the questions.**

1 Why is South Africa also called the Rainbow Nation?

2 Why are there so many marine species around South Africa?

3 What's special about the wildlife in South Africa?

4 **Find the adverbs in the text. What adjective does each one describe? What noun does each adverb–adjective combination describe?**

particularly exceptionally incredibly slightly surprisingly amazingly

Listening

5 7.9 **Listen to the first part of a Cape Town walking tour. Are the sentences true or false?**

1 Cape Town is the oldest city in South Africa.

2 You can get to Table Mountain by cable car.

3 The harbour is an industrial area of Cape Town.

4 Robben Island was used a prison for three centuries.

6 7.10 **Listen to the second part of the tour. Complete the information.**

ROBBEN ISLAND
Museum

FERRY TIMES:
9 am, 11 am, **(1)** .... and **(2)** ....

LEAVES FROM:
(3) .... Gateway

TICKETS:
adults R200 / children **(4)** R............

TOUR INCLUDES:
a **(5)** .... trip across Table Bay, a visit to the Maximum Security Prison and a **(6)** .... tour of the Island.

History and English

The human journey

1 **Look at the map. Find the part of the world where you live. When did humans first arrive there?**

2 **Read the text and find two ways that scientists work out where humans came from originally.**

Every individual has a unique 'genome' – the information coded in our DNA. Our genome holds information about our history. By comparing genomes from different people around the world, biologists can see where our ancestors came from.

Now, as part of research into this subject, South African Archbishop Desmond Tutu has had his genome deciphered. In the same study, four tribal leaders from southern Africa have also had their genomes sequenced. One of the things the study revealed is that the tribesmen have a gene that makes a high-fat diet more likely to cause them health problems. The information has been added to a database, GenBank. This is an open, public database that scientists can consult for their research.

In the past, the ideas we had about our origins came from fossils and other archaeological studies. Scientists believed that humans inhabited Africa first and then spread out to the other continents. Now, by comparing the DNA in the chromosomes of people from different areas of the world and fossil DNA, genetic evidence proves that this theory is correct.

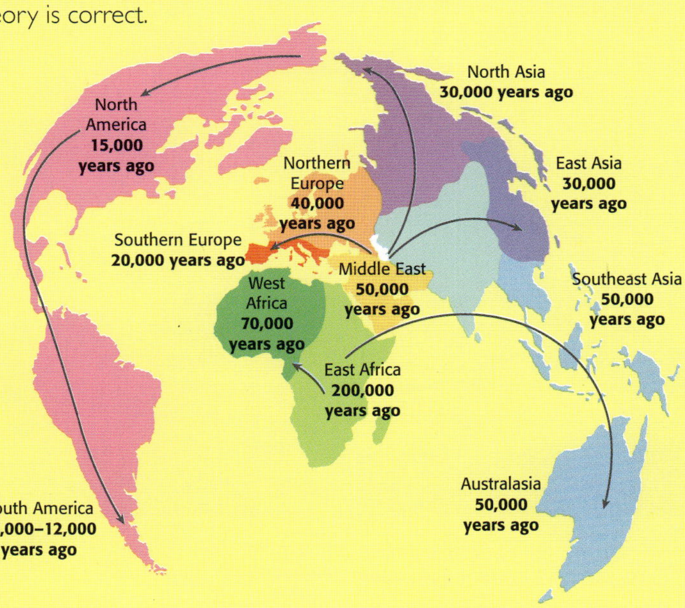

3 **What other useful information can our genome give us?**

Project

Choose a famous person from the field of science or politics in your country. Ask six people what they think about the person. Prepare a presentation about the person's achievements and how they are viewed today.

John Glenn

1 Read the article below and say what happened on the dates in the timeline.

1921
1957
1962
1963
1998

John Glenn was born in Ohio on July 18, 1921. He was awarded several medals during World War II and the Korean War and reached **the rank of colonel**. In 1957, he became the first person to fly from California to New York going **faster than the speed of sound**. When the US space programme began, Glenn was chosen as one of the very first astronauts. In 1962, Glenn flew in the first American spaceship to orbit the Earth – Friendship 7.

Glenn was a friend of President Kennedy and, although **he could have continued in the field of space exploration**, Glenn decided to enter the world of politics after Kennedy's death in 1963. Glenn later went on to spend 24 years in the **US Senate**, during which time, Glenn had a series of victories and defeats in the political world.

In 1998, Glenn retired from politics and, aged 77. **If he had disappeared from public life** at that point, Glenn would have always been remembered as a hero. However, **with a lifetime of achievements behind him**, Glenn did something even more remarkable. He became the oldest man to go into space.

Scientists wanted to study the effects of space travel on older people, and Glenn was the perfect man for the job. During the mission, Glenn's brain, heart and lungs were all carefully monitored. The results will give us a deeper knowledge of the effects of aging here on Earth, and help us to deal with many health problems faced by older people.

John Glenn showed the world what one man was capable of in a lifetime. Soldier, pilot, space explorer, politician and medical researcher – how many people can claim to have done so much with their life?

On two occasions during the war, Glenn returned to base with over 200 holes in his aircraft.

....

There is a film, *The Right Stuff*, about the first seven astronauts in the US space programme. Actor Ed Harris plays the part of Glenn.

....

'The most important thing we can do is inspire young minds and to advance the kind of science, math and technology education that will help youngsters take us to the next phase of space travel.'
John Glenn

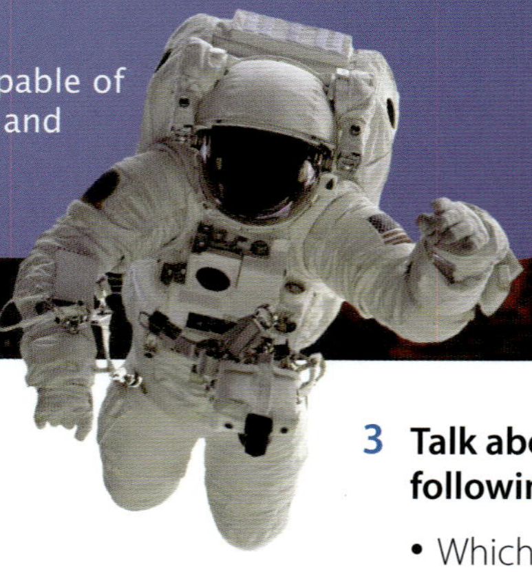

2 Choose the correct answers based on your understanding of the article

Paragraph 1

1 The *rank of colonel* is something which **most / few** soldiers reach.

2 Going *faster than the speed of sound* was **common / uncommon** in 1957.

Paragraph 2

3 *He could have continued in the field of space exploration* suggests he **had / didn't have** the opportunity.

4 The *US Senate* is probably a **political / scientific** organisation.

Paragraph 3

5 *If he had disappeared from public life* suggests that he **did / didn't** disappear.

6 *With a lifetime of achievements behind him* suggests that he **had done a lot / had more to do**.

3 Talk about one or more of the following questions with a partner.

- Which of Glenn's achievements do you admire the most?
- Would you be prepared to take part in a space exploration programme? Why / Why not?
- Why do you think Glenn left the space programme to move into politics?
- Why do you think he left politics and went into space at the age of 77?
- John Glenn recently said that he was against space tourism because it had no scientific purpose. What do you think?

NATIONAL GEOGRAPHIC

8 Shopping

> Grammar

Learn about reported statements and questions.

> Vocabulary

Learn words for shops and services, and words connected with money.

Work with reporting verbs, and word combinations with *money*.

> Skills

Read about a surprising scientific discovery, spending, and shopping online.

Listen to someone doing a shopping questionnaire, and to a telephone conversation following an online purchase.

Write a formal letter.

> Communicate

Return things to shops.

1 Look at the photo. Complete the sentence in as many ways as you can.

The girl has been …

2 Work in pairs. You have two minutes. Write things you can buy in the places in the vocabulary box. Now compare your list with a new partner.

baker's	butcher's	greengrocer's	newsagent's	post office
bank	chemist's	hairdresser's	shoe shop	travel agency
bookshop	florist's	library	supermarket	

3 8.1 Write questions for a survey about shopping habits. Then listen and check your questions.

1 what / favourite shops?
2 where / like going?
3 who / usually go with?
4 you / always know what you want?

4 8.1 Listen again and tick the answer the person gives.

1	a	clothes	b	sports gear	c	music
2	a	small shops	b	big shops	c	shopping malls
3	a	your parents	b	your friends	c	by yourself
4	a	yes	b	no	c	it depends

5 Work in pairs. Ask and answer the questions from the survey.

8A Advertising

Advert used in UK and Ireland only

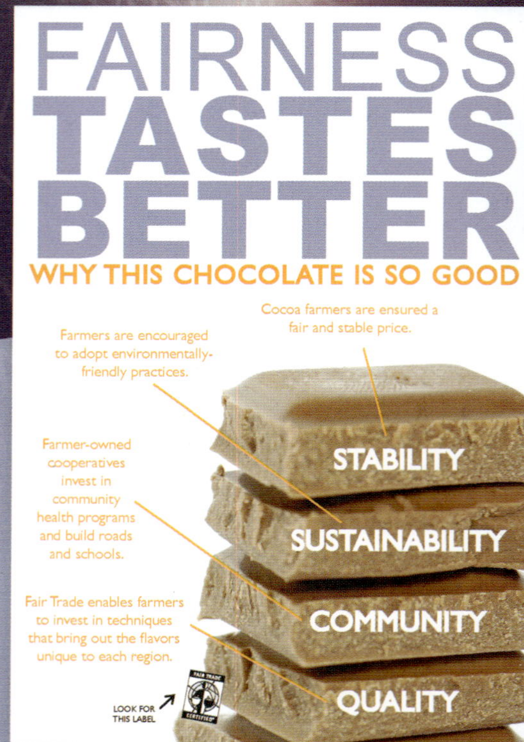

Speaking

1 **Work in pairs. Look at the two adverts and find two products and one brand.**

2 **Work in pairs. What do you think makes a good advert? Discuss these statements with reference to the two adverts.**

1. It gives me information about the product.
2. It looks good visually.
3. It makes me want to buy the product.
4. It's unusual and interesting.
5. It has a strong and clear message.

Reading and listening

3 8.2 **Read and listen to the news story. Answer the questions.**

1. What is Ribena?
2. Who are Anna Devathasan and Jenny Suo?
3. What is GSK?
4. What is *Fair Go*?

4 **Read the news story again and say if the sentences are true or false.**

1. Anna and Jenny discovered a problem with the Ribena advert.
2. GSK did not accept the girls' claims at first.
3. As a result of the girls' findings, GSK stopped selling Ribena in New Zealand.

SCHOOLGIRL SCIENTISTS IN SURPRISING DISCOVERY

Two New Zealand school girls got surprise results in their school science experiment recently. They were measuring the amount of vitamin C in a blackcurrant drink, Ribena. The manufacturer's advertising claimed that the blackcurrants in Ribena had four times the vitamin C of oranges. But the girls found that there was only a tiny amount of vitamin C in Ribena, even less than a rival brand of orange juice. The girls, Anna Devathasan and Jenny Suo, thought that they had made a mistake and that they'd been doing the experiment wrongly.

The girls contacted the manufacturers of Ribena, GlaxoSmithKline (GSK). They were told that the information in the advert referred to blackcurrants, not the product itself. Then a TV programme, *Fair Go*, said that they would broadcast the story.

At first, GSK suggested that the girls had tested the wrong product, but after another investigation GSK reported that some of their products in Australia and New Zealand were affected. They stated that they could confirm that Ribena drinks in all other markets, including the UK, contained the stated levels of vitamin C, as described on product labels. GSK said they were going to change the labels on the Australian and New Zealand products, and they invited the girls to visit their offices so that the company could thank them for bringing the problem to their attention.

Working with words: reporting verbs

5 **Look at the example. Then find six more reporting verbs in the text. One is in the passive.**

Then a TV programme, *Fair Go*, said that they would broadcast the story.

See Working with words: Page 107

Grammar: reported statements

6 Look at the example from the text. Then choose the actual word in the adverts.

The manufacturer's advertising claimed that the blackcurrants in Ribena had four times the vitamin C of oranges.

'The blackcurrants in Ribena *have / had* four times the vitamin C of oranges.'

7 How does the verb change when the words are reported?

See Grammar Explorer: Page 125

8 Read the actual words that were spoken. Then find the sentences in the text that report the words.

1. 'We've made a mistake.'
2. 'We've been doing the experiment wrongly.'
3. 'The information in the advert refers to blackcurrants.'
4. 'We will broadcast the story.'
5. 'Only some of our products in Australia and New Zealand are affected.'
6. 'We can confirm that Ribena drinks in all other markets contain the stated levels of vitamin C.'
7. 'We are going to change the labels on the Australian and New Zealand products.'

We also change pronouns when we report people's words. 'We've made a mistake.' → They thought they'd made a mistake.

9 Complete the table with the words in the box.

could did had had been were would

Direct speech	Reported speech
has	had
have	(1) ....
do	did
does	(2) ....
will	(3) ....
is	was
are	(4) ....
can	(5) ....
was	(6) ....

10 Read these comments. What did the people actually say? Write their words.

1. A government spokesman said that shoppers were showing more interest in Fairtrade values.
2. The Fairtrade director said that people could enjoy Fairtrade values with Starbucks coffee.
3. The Starbucks director said they had had a partnership with Fairtrade for over a decade.
4. A spokesman for a farmers' cooperative said they would benefit from guaranteed prices.

11 Read what an advertising executive, Marisa, says about her work. Report her words.

e.g. 'I've worked in advertising for ten years.'
Marisa said she'd worked in advertising for ten years.

1. 'A good advert is easy to understand.'
2. 'My best advert was very simple.'
3. 'I've always used humour in my adverts.'
4. 'An advert can't use misleading information.'

12 Write a sentence for each picture beginning 'The advert said ...'

1 'Megasmile will make your teeth white!'

2 '4eva glasses have a life-long guarantee.'

3 'NatureTan has been extensively tested.'

4 'Each designer shirt is totally unique.'

Speaking

13 Work in pairs. Choose four people you both know. Work alone and write something each person said yesterday. Now report the words to your partner. Can they guess the person?

A: *This person said we could go home early today.*
B: *Mrs Wilson?*

Fast finishers

Find the nine letter word. How many words can you make with the letters?

A	E	E	I	D	T	S	R	V

8B Spending money

Speaking

1 Complete the questions (1–4) with words from the vocabulary box. More than one question is possible. Then work in pairs, and ask and answer the questions. Take turns.

1 How much .... do you get every week?
2 Have you got your own .... ?
3 Have you ever used a .... ?
4 Are there any .... or .... in your pocket?

bank account **budget** **cash** **cash machine** **coin** **credit card** **debit card** **note** **pocket money** **savings** **wages**

Reading and listening

2 An interviewer asked three people about money. Read quickly what they said. Then look at the photos, and match the people (1–3) with the photos (a–c).

3 8.3 **Read and listen to what the people said again. Complete the interviewer's questions with the people's names.**

1 The interviewer asked .... if she knew how to budget.
2 .... was asked if she'd saved a lot when she was younger.
3 The interviewer asked .... if she had any credit cards.
4 .... was asked if she'd ever bought anything online.
5 The interviewer asked how much .... would spend this weekend.
6 The interviewer asked .... what she was going to spend her savings on.

1 Emma

Yes, I do, actually. My mum's shown me how to do it. I'm going to a summer camp in France this year and I'll need to make my money last for a month. So she's been helping me to work out how much I'll need for travel, for entertainment and things like that.

No, I haven't got any credit cards – I'm not old enough. When I go to France I'm going to take an emergency supply of twenty-euro notes!

2 Rachel

No, I haven't. I prefer to pay for things with cash and you can't do that on the Internet! My wages are paid directly into my bank account and I get money out of the cash machine once a week.

I'll probably spend quite a lot of money at the weekend. It's my daughter's birthday and I want to take her to London for the day.

3 Diane

No! I used to be terrible with money! I used to waste all my pocket money on sweets and rubbish every week. Once, I wanted to buy an expensive book. It was about the artwork in *Lord of the Rings*. My dad said I could have all the coins that were lying around the house. I managed to find £23.60!

These days I put all my loose change in a big jar. That's my savings. I'm waiting until the jar is full. Then I'm going to buy something amazing with what I've saved.

a

b

c

Working with words: word combinations with *money*

4 **Look at the examples. How many more combinations with *money* do you know?**

I'll probably spend quite a lot of money this weekend.

I used to be terrible with money!

See Working with words: Page 107

Grammar: reported questions

5 **Look at the example. Then write the direct questions for the reported questions.**

The interviewer asked Emma if she had a bank account.

The interviewer asked, 'Have you got a bank account?'

1 The interviewer asked Emma if she needed to buy euros.
2 The interviewer asked Rachel what they would do in London.
3 Rachel was asked if she'd ever used a cash machine.
4 Diane was asked how much money she'd saved.
5 The interviewer asked Diane what she was going to buy with her savings.

See Grammar Explorer: Page 127

We also change possessive adjectives when we report people's words, e.g. *your* → *her/his*.

6 **Report the interviewer's questions.**

e.g. 'Are you good with money?'
The interviewer asked me if I was good with money.

1 'Are you saving any money at the moment?'
2 'Where do you keep your savings?'
3 'What will you buy with your savings?'
4 'Have you ever won any money?'
5 'Did you spend a lot yesterday?'

7 **Write the questions you asked your partner in Exercise 1 as reported questions and write the replies.**

e.g. I asked Kate how much pocket money she got every week.
She said she got 50 pounds a month.

Listening

8 8.4 STUDY SKILLS **Work in pairs. Which is the best definition of a shopaholic (a–c)? Listen to someone doing a shopping questionnaire and check your answer.**

a Shopaholics go shopping more often than necessary and often buy unnecessary things.
b Shopaholics feel in control of their shopping habits and usually don't spend more than budget they set themselves.
c Shopaholics feel stressed when they are in a shop and only buy things that they've seen advertised.

9 8.4 **Listen again. Tick the questions that you heard.**

Wayne asked Charlie …

1 if he went shopping more than three times a week.
2 what his favourite shops were.
3 if he had spent more than his budget on his last shopping trip.
4 if he had ever bought more than he needed.
5 how he felt when he was shopping.
6 if he was influenced by advertising or by his friends.

Speaking

10 **Write the direct questions for the reported questions in Exercise 9.**

e.g. Do you go shopping more than three times a week?

11 **Work in pairs. Ask your partner the questions from the shopping questionnaire. Take turns.**

A: *Do you go shopping more than three times a week?*
B: *No, I don't. I usually go shopping about once a week.*

12 **Work with a new partner. Report your conversation.**

Study skills

Listening and checking

Before you listen to an exam text, read the information or the exam questions.

1 Find the key words to listen for.
2 When you listen, check for this information.
3 Don't forget that the same ideas can be expressed in different ways.

8C Returning things

Reading and listening

1 8.5 **Look at the photo. What are Dan and Holly doing? Read and listen to the dialogue and check your answer.**

2 **Read the dialogue again. Answer the questions.**

1 What is the problem with the video game?
2 What does Holly ask for?
3 What do Holly and Dan decide to do?

3 **Look at the *Useful expressions*. Write C for customer or A for assistant next to each expression.**

USEFUL EXPRESSIONS

Can I help you?
Have you got the receipt?
I'd like to return this game.
I'm afraid we don't usually give refunds.
Is there something wrong with it?
Would it be possible to get my money back?
Would you like a credit note?

4 8.6 **Listen and repeat the *Useful expressions*. Focus on your intonation.**

Assistant: Can I help you?
Dan: Yes, please. I'd like to return this game.
Assistant: I see. Is there something wrong with it?
Dan: No, no. My friend bought it for me for my birthday, but I've already got it.
Holly: I should have asked him which games he had before buying it, I suppose!
Assistant: Yes, but it's nice to try and surprise people, isn't it? Have you got the receipt?
Holly: Yes, I have. Here you are.
Assistant: Would you like a credit note, or do you want to exchange it for another game?
Holly: Would it be possible to get my money back?
Assistant: Well, I'm afraid we don't usually give refunds unless the goods are faulty.
Holly: Oh, I see.
Assistant: But a credit note is valid for six months and we have a huge range of games, CDs and DVDs. You can use it to buy anything in the shop. And you can use it online too.
Holly: What do you think, Dan?
Dan: Let's get a credit note. I'm sure I can find something I like!

5 8.7 **Listen and match the conversations (1–3) with the places (a–d). There is one extra place.**

Writing: a formal letter

1 **Read the letter and choose the correct option (a–c).**

- a Fay is asking for information.
- b Fay is making a complaint.
- c Fay is making a suggestion.

2 **Read again and put this information in the correct sequence.**

1. an explanation of another problem
2. an explanation of the problem
3. Fay's response to the first problem
4. the reason for writing the letter
5. what action Fay requests

3 **Look at the expressions in red in the letter. Then choose the correct option.**

1. **In spite of / Because of** the terrible service, I don't buy anything from that website.
2. The shoes were really expensive. **In spite of that, / Because of that,** I bought them.
3. The website sold cheap DVDs. **Despite the price, / Because of the price,** the quality was good.
4. The film got an Oscar. **Despite this, / Because of this,** I didn't think it was very good.

Speaking

6 **Match the items with the problems. More than one match is possible.**

a CD	the wrong size
a pair of earrings	the wrong format
a T-shirt	faulty
a DVD	broken
a webcam	past its sell-by date
some cheese	you already have one

7 **Work in pairs. You are a shop assistant and a customer. Write dialogues about the things in Exercise 6. Use the *Useful expressions* to help you. Then take a role each and practise your dialogues.**

Pronunciation: syllable stress

8 8.8 **Listen to the words. Which syllables are stressed? Listen again and repeat the pairs of words.**

1. a refund — to refund
2. advertise — advertisement
3. advertise — advertising
4. democracy — democratic
5. investigate — investigation
6. politics — politician
7. qualified — qualification

4 **Write a letter of complaint. Use an example from your own experience, or invent a product and a problem. Use Fay's letter to help you.**

Dear Sir / Madam,

I am writing to complain about the service from your website.

Two months ago, I ordered three DVDs from you. The information on the website said they were for Europe (Region 2). Despite this, when they arrived, they were for Region 1. I returned the DVDs to you with a note explaining what had happened and asking for a refund.

In spite of my letter, you have sent me the wrong items again, this time the Blu-ray versions of the titles.

Please could you refund my PayPal account or send me the correct (Region 2) format DVDs. I enclose the receipt.

Yours faithfully,

Fay Johnson

8D Shopping online in the UK

Reading

1 **Look at the photos. What do you think they show?**

2 **Work in pairs and discuss these questions.**

1. Do you buy things online? Why? / Why not?
2. Do you have your own money? Where or who does it come from?
3. What do you spend most money on?

3 8.9 **Read the text. Check your answers to Exercise 1. Then compare your answers to Exercise 2 with what it says in the text.**

4 **Find the following expressions in the text. Which ones mean the same thing?**

apart from as well as except for
in addition to instead of

Culture

What kind of shop would you go to if you wanted to buy an Apollo 17 spacesuit? Or a swimming pool? Or a UFO detector? Can you even buy such things? Just go online and do a search. You can order them all on the Internet.

Is there anything you can't buy online these days? Internet shopping has changed enormously from the days when there was nothing to buy apart from books. Nowadays, you can find everything from virtual florists to virtual shoe shops on the Internet. Who does most online shopping? Teenagers don't usually have much money to spend, but despite this they make up an increasing number of online consumers. A few years ago, there was no way of paying for e-shopping except for credit cards, which teenagers don't own. But now, as well as using credit cards, you can use debit cards, systems like PayPal and store cards to pay for your purchases.

So what do British teenagers buy online? Well, almost all of the things they spend their money on can be bought over the Internet. A recent survey reported that the most popular purchases are music, computer games, mobile phone credit and ring tones, fashion, cosmetics and sports gear. These days, most teens download music instead of going to a 'real' record store. With the new payments systems, it's just as easy to buy a single online as it is to download a ring tone to a phone. Of course, teenagers rely mostly on their parents for their income, (apart from some aged 15 and over who earn money from a part-time job). In addition to this, most teenagers prefer money instead of a gift for a birthday or Christmas.
In general, young people in the UK today have a lot more cash than their parents did when they were young, and there are many more things to spend it on.

5 Rewrite the sentences using expressions from Exercise 4.

1 I download albums and singles online.
2 I buy books online. I don't go to a bookshop.
3 I don't buy much online, only music.
4 I use PayPal and credit cards to buy things online.
5 I don't like many shops. I like clothes shops.

Listening

6 8.10 **Listen to the telephone conversation following an online purchase. Complete the missing information.**

1 item ....
2 problem ....
3 reference number ....
4 payment method ....
5 price ....

Project

Design a survey to find out what your classmates spend their money on. Ask the questions and present the results as a chart or diagram. Write a short text to accompany the diagram.

Maths and English

Statistics

1 Work in pairs. Do you know what a 'pie chart' is? Look at the text and check your answer.

2 Read the text and do the activities. Compare your answers with your partner.

Statistics is the part of maths which deals with using information that is expressed in numbers. This information is often called 'data'. Data can be shown in the form of tables, graphs, charts and other diagrams. This is a useful way of making the key information clear. However, charts and diagrams usually present a summary of the main information – they don't explain the details of the information.

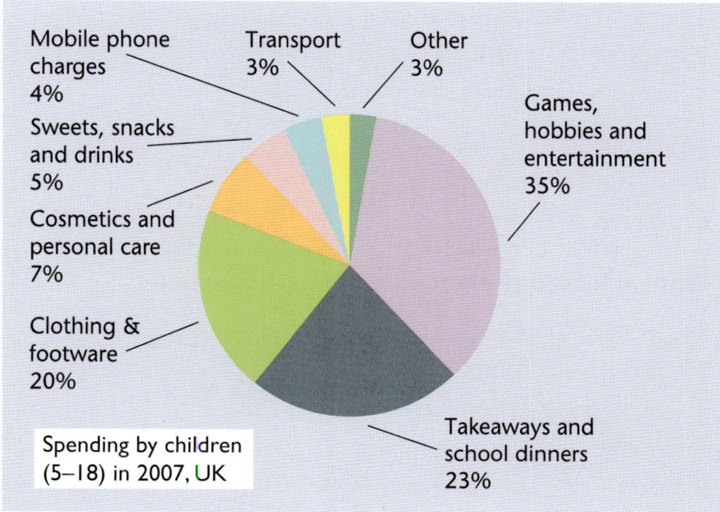

Spending by children (5–18) in 2007, UK

Activity 1 What do the percentages in the pie chart add up to? Why?

Activity 2 Look at the pie chart carefully. Then read the information below. Which data is also shown in the pie chart?

1 In 2007, children aged five to 18 spent most on games, hobbies and entertainment.
2 This category includes spending on music, computer games and DVDs.
3 On average, children spent about £13 a week, although 13 to 15-year-olds spent over £20 a week compared to much less for younger children.
4 Children spent 23 per cent of their total spending on meals and a much smaller amount on sweets and snacks.
5 About 4 per cent of total spending was on mobile phone charges, but this was accounted for only by children over 11.
6 About 20 per cent of spending was on clothes and footwear.
7 Girls spent about double the amount that boys did on clothes. Young teenage boys, on the other hand, spent about five times as much as girls on games and hobbies.

3 Does any of the information in the pie chart surprise you? Explain why.

Consolidation Units 7 and 8

Reading

Identifying the writer's purpose

- Read the text and the options quickly.
- Think about typical expressions that express the functions described in the options. Look for these in the text.
- **Important!** You don't need to understand every word in the text to be able to do the task.

1 Match the sentences (1–3) with the functions (a–c).

1 I went out to do some shopping.
2 You didn't go out, did you?
3 You shouldn't have gone out.

a checking information
b making a criticism
c giving a reason

2 Write at least one expression for each function.

1 inviting somebody to do something
2 asking for information
3 expressing an opinion
4 apologising for something
5 expressing a preference
6 asking for advice
7 making a complaint
8 making a recommendation
9 expressing regret

3 Read the note and choose the expressions that match functions in Exercise 2.

> Hi Jen,
> How are you today? I'm really sorry about last night. I was in a bad mood, but I know that's no excuse for my behaviour. I shouldn't have shouted. Please accept my apologies. Can we talk about it? I'll call you later.
> Anna

4 Choose the correct option (a–c).

Read Anna's note. Why has she written to Jen?

a to apologise
b to ask for help
c to give advice

5 Match these expressions (a–f) with six of the functions (1–9) in Exercise 2 in the left-hand column.

a What do you think I should do?
b I'm really sorry about that.
c Would you like to go for a burger?
d I wish I hadn't told you.
e Could you tell me where the bookshop is?
f The film seemed a bit boring to me.

6 Read each statement and choose the best option (a–c).

1 You are in a shop. You want to know the price of a camera. What do you say?
   a I'd like to return this camera.
   b Can I help you?
   c Could you tell me how much this is, please?

2 You lent your friend a DVD. He says he didn't enjoy it. How do you respond?
   a Why do you say that?
   b What did you think of it?
   c Because I liked it.

3 You answer a phone call for your sister. She's not at home. What do you say?
   a Can you take a message?
   b Can I leave a message?
   c Can I take a message?

wish + past simple

wish + past simple refers to situations in the present.

I wish they had this shirt in yellow.

1 Look at the picture above. Which sentence (a or b) is true?

a The shop hasn't got the colour he wants.
b The shop has got the shirt in yellow.

2 Complete the sentences with the correct form of the verb.

1 I wish it ………… (**be**) cheaper.
2 I wish I ………… (**like**) green.
3 I wish it ………… (**not have**) a round neck.

wish + past perfect

wish + past perfect refers to situations in the past.

I wish I'd tried this on in the shop.

3 Look at the picture above. Which sentence (a or b) is true?

a He tried the jacket on before he bought it.
b He bought the jacket without trying it on first.

4 Complete the sentences with the correct form of the verb.

1 I wish I ………… (**buy**) a smaller size.
2 I wish I ………… (**not be**) in a hurry.
3 I wish you ………… (**come**) with me.

5 Complete the table with the verbs.

isn't had been was wasn't

situation in the present	I wish the shirt (**1**) ………… cheaper, but it (**2**) ………… .
situation in the past	I wish the shirt (**3**) ………… cheaper, but it (**4**) ………… .

6 Read each sentence or each pair of sentences. Say if *I wish* refers to the past (PA) or the present (PR).

1 I wish I'd seen the advert. Then I would have known about the offer. …………
2 I wish my local shop sold Fairtrade products. …………
3 I wish you'd bought Fairtrade chocolate. It tastes great and the farmers get more money. …………
4 I wish I didn't have to go shopping. There's a great match on TV. …………
5 I wish the sales were on. I'm short of money. …………
6 I wish you'd asked me – I would have lent you some money. …………

7 Read the first sentence and complete the second sentence.

1 These Nike trainers are too expensive for me. (**wish / cheaper**)
2 When I went to the bank yesterday, it was shut. (**wish / know**)
3 They only sell that version of the film online. (**wish / have a PayPal account**)
4 I didn't know the Top Shop sale finished yesterday! (**wish / you tell me**)
5 I don't get much pocket money. (**wish / get more**)
6 I'd love to buy this DVD. (**wish / more money**)

8 Look at the picture. Write sentences with *I wish* and the ideas from the box or ideas of your own. Write three sentences you would say during the match and three sentences you would say after the match.

be a Chelsea supporter
be in the crowd
play better
score more goals
Porto win
Porto have a better goalkeeper

Review Units 7 and 8

Vocabulary

1 Write the words. They are all nouns.

1 a place where scientists work l............
2 investigating something r............
3 a scientific idea t............
4 finding something new d............
5 a piece of equipment m............

1 mark per item: .../5 marks

2 Complete the paragraph with words about politics.

In a country that is a (**1**) d............ , there are (**2**) e............ to choose a new (**3**) g............ . At this time, people can (**4**) v............ for the politician they prefer. In most countries, everyone over the age of 18 has the (**5**) r............ to participate.

1 mark per item: .../5 marks

3 Write the places where you can buy the things.

1 ....
2 ....
3 ....
4 ....
5 ....

1 mark per item: .../5 marks

4 Complete the sentences.

1 When the bank is closed, we use the c............ m............ .
2 My mum gives me £5 p............ m............ every Friday.
3 I need a job that pays better w............ .
4 I save all my 20-pence c............ in a jar.
5 You can't have a c............ c............ until you are 18 years old.

1 mark per item: .../5 marks

5 Write verbs that have the opposite meanings.

1 connect ....
2 lock ....
3 agree ....
4 pack ....
5 encode ....

1 mark per item: .../5 marks

Grammar

6 Complete the endings of the third conditional sentence.

If I had got up earlier this morning, ...

1 I .... (**eat**) breakfast.
2 I .... (**not / be**) late for school.
3 we .... (**walk**) to school together.
4 I .... (**not / miss**) the French exam.
5 I .... (**not have to**) see the head teacher.

1 mark per item: .../5 marks

7 Complete the endings of the third conditional sentence.

The experiment would have worked if ...

1 we .... (**follow**) the instructions.
2 you .... (**not / use**) the wrong chemical.
3 I .... (**listen**) to the teacher.
4 we .... (**not / be**) in a hurry.
5 the teacher .... (**help**) us.

1 mark per item: .../5 marks

8 Complete the sentences with *could, couldn't, should* or *shouldn't*.

1 I'm sorry I'm late. I .... have phoned.
2 If I'd known you were going shopping, we .... have gone together.
3 You .... have said that. It wasn't nice.
4 You .... have asked me before you borrowed my phone!
5 Don't worry! You .... have helped – we needed an expert.

1 mark per item: .../5 marks

9 Report the words. Begin with *She said ...*.

1 'It's an excellent product.'
2 'I saw the advert on TV.'
3 'I've been to that shop a few times.'
4 'We'll be home at 8 p.m.'
5 'John can't come to dinner.'

1 mark per item: .../5 marks

10 Report the questions. Begin with *He asked ...*.

1 'Where are you going?'
2 'Do you read many magazines?'
3 'Will you be at home on Sunday?'
4 'Have you finished work?'
5 'Where did you go at the weekend?'

1 mark per item: .../5 marks

Communicate

11 Match the statements (1–5) with the follow-up comments (a–e).

1 I can't do this homework.
2 I forgot my mum's birthday.
3 It's too late to go shopping now.
4 My friend is upset with me.
5 There are no tickets left!

a I shouldn't have argued with her.
b I wish I'd asked the teacher for help.
c I wish we'd got here earlier.
d I wish I'd looked at the time earlier.
e I should have written it on the calendar.

2 marks per item: .../10 marks

12 Complete the dialogue with the expressions.

can I help you · have you got the receipt · I'm afraid · we'd like to return · would you like

Assistant: Good morning, (**1**) .... ?
Lee: Yes, (**2**) .... this DVD.
Assistant: OK, it hasn't been opened. That's fine. (**3**) .... ?
Lee: Yes, we have. Here you are.
Assistant: OK, is there another DVD you want?
Lee: We haven't looked, actually.
Assistant: (**4**) .... a credit note, instead?
Lee: Would it be possible to get my money back?
Assistant: Well, (**5**) .... we don't usually give refunds.
Lee: Oh well, I suppose we can choose something. Let's have a look.

2 marks per item: .../10 marks

13 Which letter is silent in each word?

1 bomb ....
2 castle ....
3 could ....
4 design ....
5 doubt ....
6 foreign ....
7 half ....
8 island ....
9 know ....
10 scientific ....

1 mark per item: .../10 marks

14 Complete the sentences with these words.

before · despite that · except for · in spite of · without

1 We solved the problem .... asking for help.
2 .... deciding to buy the GPS, we looked at the price.
3 .... the bad weather, lots of people came to our picnic.
4 I don't like any fruit .... bananas.
5 My camera was cheap, but .... it takes great photos.

2 marks per item: .../10 marks

15 Complete the letter with these words.

about · after · as · because · for · if · in · to · us · when

Dear Sir / Madam,
I am writing to complain (**1**) .... the service in your shop. We went there last Saturday (**2**) .... my son wanted (**3**) .... buy a games console. (**4**) .... waiting for at least ten minutes, an assistant served us. My son asked him several questions about the console he was interested (**5**) .... , but the assistant didn't know anything. (**6**) .... well as this, he was quite impolite.

He told (**7**) .... to read the information leaflet (**8**) .... we wanted to know about the consoles. (**9**) .... I asked to speak to the manager, the assistant disappeared and did not return. We then left the shop.

We have been customers at your shop (**10**) .... many years, but I'm afraid we will not return in the future.
Yours,
Mr D. Harris

2 marks per item: .../20 marks

Total: .../100

I can...

I can talk about regrets.
I can make criticisms.
I can return things to shops

1 Working with words

verb + preposition *at, to*

Some verbs are followed by prepositions.

She's staring at the poster.

He's waving to the crowd.

1 Write *at* or *to* in the correct place in the table.

explain (something) to	speak ....
laugh at	stare at
listen	talk to
look	throw at
point (something) at	throw to
shout at	wave to
shout to	write ....

2 Complete the sentences with *at* or *to*.

1 What are you looking .... ?
2 My best friend isn't speaking .... me.
3 Don't point your finger .... me!
4 Do you talk .... your pets?

3 Complete the sentences with verb + preposition combinations from the table in Exercise 1.

1 What kind of music do you like .... ?
2 How often do you .... your penfriend ?
3 Do you .... funny TV shows?
4 Can you .... this exercise .... me?

4 Work in pairs. Ask and answer the questions in Exercise 3.

Different prepositions can change the meaning.
For example:
You shout at somebody when you are angry.
You shout to somebody to get their attention.

5 Choose the correct preposition.

1 Our teacher never shouts **at** / **to** us.
2 Shout **at** / **to** Joe. Tell him we're going home.
3 Can I borrow your pen? Throw it **at** / **to** me.
4 Stop throwing stones **at** / **to** the window!

Working on your own

6 Write your own sentence with each verb + preposition combination.

apologise to **describe something / somebody to**
have a look at

noun + noun

We can use two nouns together to make another noun. This is called a compound noun. A compound noun can be one word or two.

autograph + book =
autograph book

news + paper =
newspaper

1 Match these nouns to make compound nouns.

phone	guard
security	line
soap	opera
talent	show

2 Complete the compound nouns in the table with these words.

club guest line review site

autograph book	music/TV/film ....
celebrity	newspaper
camera bag	rubbish tip
detective story	shop assistant
fan	slideshow
fashion design	sports report
film location	summer clothes
head............	survival kit
horseshoe	web............
message board	world champion
mind control	
museum official	

3 Look at the compound nouns in Exercises 1 and 2 and find the names of these things.

1

2
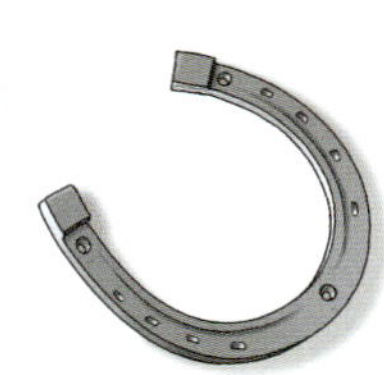

3

4

Working on your own

4 Choose four compound nouns from the tables in Exercises 1 and 2. Write your own sentence with each compound noun.

2 Working with words

abstract nouns

Abstract nouns are things you can't see or touch. They can be things like states, feelings and qualities.

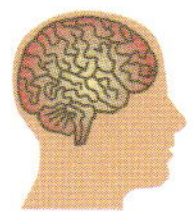

You can see a brain.

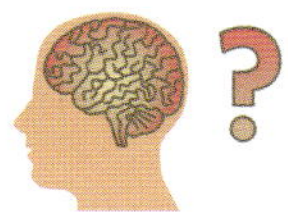

You can't see a mind.

1 Write the nouns in the correct place in the table.

advice feeling idea information luck

Uncountable		Countable
....	imagination	ambition
anger	....	danger
behaviour	intelligence	fear
communication	logic	....
creativity	love	friendship
education	....	....
happiness	sadness	memory
hate	truth	mind
health	wealth	strength
hypnosis		success
		superstition
		thought

We usually use most countable abstract nouns in the singular: *danger, fear, memory.*

2 Choose the correct option.

1 He never remembers birthdays. He's got a terrible **logic / memory**.
2 The scientist has investigated animal **idea / intelligence**.
3 You write good stories. You have a lot of **imagination / thought**.
4 Some scientists study animal **behaviour / superstition**.

3 What do people feel in each situation? Write a word from the table in Exercise 1.

1 A tiger is coming towards you.
2 It's the first day of the holidays.
3 You've made the same mistake three times.
4 Two people you know are getting married.
5 You watch a film where the hero dies.

Working on your own

4 Write the translations of these abstract nouns.

friendship strength truth wealth

verb + *-ing*

We can add *-ing* to a verb to give the name of an activity.

smoke + *ing* = smoking

park + *ing* = parking

1 Add *-ing* to these verbs and write them in the table. Be careful with the spelling.

dance make rescue swim

camping	parking
carrying (something)	practising
cooking	public speaking
counting (something)	pulling (something)
....	repeating (something)
drawing	....
fishing	riding
fixing (something)	singing
flying	smoking
frightening (somebody)	....
hunting	swinging (something)
.... notes	telling jokes
memorising words	watching (something)
painting	

2 Complete the lists with expressions from the table in Exercise 1. Use each expression once only.

1 ways of hypnotising people: counting, ...
2 ways of learning English: memorising words, ... , ... , ...
3 things people can be frightened of: .... , ...
4 free-time activities: camping, ... , ... , ... , ...
5 things animals can be good at: carrying something, ... , ...
6 things people can be good at: cooking, ... , ... , ...

3 Complete the sentences so that they are true for you. Then compare with your partner.

1 I'm quite good at ....
2 I've never been ....
3 .... is fun.
4 I'm (not) frightened of ....

Working on your own

4 Choose three verbs from the table in Exercise 1 and write sentences.

3 Working with words

verb + *to* + infinitive

Some verbs are followed by *to* and the infinitive of another verb.

They decided to leave.

She agreed to sing for them.

1 Add the verbs in the examples above to the table.

....	hope to	pretend to
begin to	learn to	refuse to
....	manage to	seem to
force to	need to	want to
help to	prefer to	

2 Choose the correct option.

1 Archaeology **needs to** / **helps to** explain how our ancestors lived.

2 It was snowing a lot. We **decided to** / **hoped to** make a snowman.

3 It was difficult, but I **managed to** / **seemed to** speak French.

4 I had no transport. My friend **preferred to** / **agreed to** lend me his bike.

3 Complete the questions about childhood with verbs from the table in Exercise 1.

1 What did you .... to be when you were little?

2 When did you .... to ride a bike?

3 Did you ever .... to eat food you didn't like?

4 Did your dad .... to be Santa Claus at Christmas?

4 Work in pairs. Ask and answer the questions in Exercise 3.

5 Write sentences about your own or your partner's answers to the questions in Exercise 3.

e.g. *When I was little, I wanted to be a train driver.*

Working on your own

6 Write five sentences with verbs from the table in Exercise 1. Write the translations.

American English

American English and British English sometimes have different words for the same thing.

a mobile / a cellphone

chips / fries

1 Decide which words in the pairs are American English and write them in the table.

break time / recess **gas / petrol**

apartment	fries	....
cellphone	....	sidewalk
cookie	mailman	sneakers
diner	Mom	store
drugstore	pants	trash can
elevator	parking lot	vacation
eraser	principal	

2 Find the American English words in the table in Exercise 1 for these British English words.

biscuit **flat** **head teacher** **holiday**
pavement **postman** **restaurant** **shop**

3 Look at the table and find the names of these things. What are the British English names?

1

4

2

5

3

Working on your own

4 We use the words *gas, pants, recess* and *store* in British English, but the meaning is different. Find the British English meanings in your dictionary.

4 Working with words

adjective + *to* + infinitive

Adjectives are sometimes followed by *to* and the infinitive of a verb.

This is impossible to do!

It's good to see you again!

1 Which adjectives in the table can also be used in the examples above?

amazed to	funny to	lovely to
dangerous to	good to	nice to
difficult to	happy to	pleased to
easy to	hard to	sad to
entertaining to	horrified to	surprising to
exciting to	impossible to	unusual to
fascinating to	interesting to	

2 Match the beginnings of the sentences (1–4) with the endings (a–d).

1 The game was exciting
2 That book on sport was really interesting
3 My grandad is fascinating
4 Usain Bolt is so fast he's impossible

a to beat.
b to read.
c to talk to.
d to watch.

3 Complete the sentences with these adjectives.

dangerous happy sad unusual

1 I'm .... to help you.
2 It's too .... to swim in this river.
3 I'm .... to hear you can't come too.
4 It's .... to see snakes here.

4 Write three things you find …

1 easy to do
2 hard to do
3 difficult to understand
4 entertaining to watch

5 Write four sentences with your ideas from Exercise 4.

e.g. I think crosswords are hard to do.

Working on your own

6 Write four sentences beginning *It's* … and *I'm* … with adjectives from the table in Exercise 1.

verb + noun

There are some verbs and nouns that we often use together.

'Have a look at this website.'

'I've got a degree.'

1 Write the nouns in the correct place in the table.

idea job mistake race

Verb	Noun
drive	a bus, a car, a vehicle
get	an answer, a degree, help, information, a .... , a pet, a present, a qualification
have	an accident, an argument, a career, a future, a good time, an .... , an influence, a look (at something), a meal, an operation, an opportunity, a problem
make	a decision, a film, the headlines, a meal, a .... , money, notes, things
score	a goal, a point
spend	hours, money, time
win	a championship, a competition, a game, a medal, a prize, a ....

2 Cover the table in Exercise 1. Match these verbs and nouns. Check your answers in the table.

drive	a career	get	a decision
have	help	make	hours
spend	a vehicle		

3 Complete the sentences with *get* or *have*.

1 .... a good time at the party!
2 When did you .... your dog?
3 We asked but didn't .... an answer.
4 Tell me if you .... a problem.

4 Complete the sentences with verbs from the table in Exercise 1.

1 My dad .... things from wood.
2 I .... a lot of time on my homework.
3 How many medals did you .... ?
4 My team always .... the most points.
5 Did Tim Burton .... this film?

Working on your own

5 Write sentences with verb + noun combinations when you learn them.

5 Working with words

adjective order

Adjectives before a noun usually have a specific order.

a black plastic camera   a big old car

1 Look at the five groups of adjectives. Match the headings with the groups (1–5).

age   colour   material   origin   size

1 .... : big, enormous, huge, immense, large, massive, short, tall
2 .... : ancient, new, old
3 .... : black, grey, pink-coloured, white
4 .... : American, Australian, British, Egyptian
5 .... : brick, concrete, gold, metal, plastic, silk, stone, wool

Adjectives which give factual information are used in the order (1–5) shown in Exercise 1.

2 Look at the sentences. Are the adjectives in the correct order?

1 My school is an enormous brick building.
2 I've got a plastic blue ruler.
3 Do you need this old metal box?
4 This is an Egyptian ancient pyramid.

Adjectives of shape go after adjectives of size and age, but before adjectives of colour, origin and material.

3 Write the adjectives in the correct order.

1 a box (square shaped, plastic)
2 a mirror (oval, metal)
3 a building (round, tall)
4 a sculpture (concrete, triangular)

Working on your own

4 Write a description of two things you own. Use these ideas or your own ideas.

a bicycle   a jacket   a mobile phone
a pair of boots   some jewellery

verb + preposition

Some verbs are followed by prepositions.

'I suffer from hay fever.'   'I don't believe in UFOs.'

1 Write *about, as* and *for* in the correct place in the table.

apologise for	suffer from
appeal to	talk about
ask about	think ....
ask for	translate into
believe in	use as
compete in	use for
complain about	use in
exchange for	value ....
look for	value at
make from	vote for
make into	wait for
pay	work as
rely on	work for
separate (something) from (something)	

2 Complete the questions with prepositions.

1 What's silk made .... ?
2 Which objects can you make copper .... ?
3 What did the Egyptians exchange gold .... ?
4 Which industries is gold used .... ?

3 Complete the sentences with different verbs.

1 Who did you .... for on *Dancing on Ice*?
2 Hurry up! We can't .... for you!
3 Did you .... for anything special for your birthday?
4 Can you help me .... for my keys? I've lost them.

4 Complete the sentences with prepositions.

1 My mum works .... a jewellery company.
2 My dad works .... an accountant.
3 Is this website translated .... English?
4 My sister's competing .... a race.

Working on your own

5 Write your own sentence with each verb + preposition combination.

apologise for   complain about   rely on   use for

6 Working with words

phrasal verbs

Phrasal verbs have two parts: a verb and a particle. The meaning is usually different from the meaning of the two parts on their own.
'No thanks, I'm giving up chocolate.'
He's running away from the dog.

1 Look at the sentences above and write the prepositions in the correct place in the table.

break out	get back	take off
build up	give	throw away
carry on	hand in	try out
come back	run	turn into
find out	run out	turn up
get away	set up	work out

2 Read the first sentence. Then choose the correct option.

1 I can't work out the answer to this sum.
I can't **calculate** / **describe** it.
2 I waited for ages, but the bus didn't turn up.
It didn't **leave** / **come**.
3 Oh, no! We've run out of petrol!
We've **used** / **bought** it all.
4 Let's get away from this noise!
Let's **stay here** / **go to a different place**.

3 Complete the sentences with the correct preposition or verb.

1 I got .... from my holidays yesterday.
2 Have you handed .... your homework?
3 How can we .... out the answer?
4 Do you know how to .... up a website on the Internet?

4 Complete the sentences with phrasal verbs from the table in Exercise 1.

1 What does water .... when it boils?
2 What time does your plane .... ?
3 It's hard, but we'll .... to the end.
4 Don't .... paper – recycle it!

Working on your own

5 Write your own sentences to show the meaning of each phrasal verb.

break out   build up   come back   try out

noun + preposition

Some nouns, especially abstract nouns, are followed by prepositions.
There's no difference between them.
He's had an argument with his sister.

1 Write *for*, *of* and *to* in the correct place in the table.

answer	influence on
argument with	map ....
cause of	photo of
connection between	problem with
contact with	reaction to
cure for	reason for
damage to	recipe for
decision about	reply to
difference between	research into
explanation	success with
idea of	version of

2 Complete the sentences with the correct preposition.

1 The storm did some damage .... our house.
2 Are you in contact .... your cousins?
3 Everyone has a different reaction .... Damien Hirst's paintings.
4 We don't know the cause .... the accident.

3 Cover the table in Exercise 1. Complete the sentences with the correct preposition. Then check your answers.

about   of   to   with

1 How do I send a reply .... this email?
2 I've made a decision .... my future.
3 I've got a problem .... my computer.
4 I'd like a photo .... you.

4 Complete the sentences with the correct noun.

1 Have you got a .... for banana cake?
2 There is still no .... for AIDS.
3 What's the .... for your decision to give up chocolate?

Working on your own

5 Write two nouns which are followed by each of these prepositions.

between   of   to   with

7 Working with words

prefixes

Some verbs can have prefixes such as *en-* or *de-* which give them a different meaning.

They rebuilt the city after the earthquake.

1 Look at the example and write the infinitive of the verb in the table.

decipher decode	enable encode encrypt endanger enlarge	undo unlock unpack
disable disagree disappear disconnect	reappear .... recreate redo rename rewrite	

2 Find verbs in the table in Exercise 1 which have opposite meanings to these verbs.

agree appear decode enable lock

3 Choose the correct option.

1. We arrived at the hotel and **packed** / **unpacked** our suitcases.
2. We can **create** / **recreate** Fleming's experiments today.
3. My project was terrible. I'm going to **write** / **rewrite** it.
4. I need to print something. How do I **connect** / **disconnect** the printer?

4 Cover the table in Exercise 1. Write verbs that have these meanings. Then check your answers.

1. give something a new name
2. do something again
3. put someone in danger
4. make something bigger

Working on your own

5 Write sentences to show the difference between these verb pairs.

enable / disable undo / redo
disappear / reappear

suffixes

We can add suffixes to verbs and nouns to make nouns and adjectives.
inform – information
qualify – qualification

1 Complete the words in the table.

Verb	Noun	Adjective
advertise	advertise............ advertising	
	archaeology archaeologist	archaeological
comfort	comfort	comfort............
communicate	communication	
compete	compet............	competitive
create	creativity	creative
	democracy	democratic
elect	election	
govern	government	
	happiness	happy
inform	inform............	informative
	intelligence	intelligent
investigate	investigation	
	politics politician	political
qualify	qualification	qualified
save	savings	

2 Find words in the table for these things.

1. a person who works in politics
2. something detectives do
3. a good feeling
4. a group of people who lead a country

3 Choose the correct option.

1. That's a really funny **advertisement** / **advertising**.
2. Good leaders **communicate** / **communication** well.
3. Animals can be **creativity** / **creative**.
4. Who will win the **elect** / **election**?
5. Are you interested in **political** / **politics**?

Working on your own

4 Write nouns and/or adjectives from these words.

decide free know science

8 Working with words

reporting verbs

We can use different verbs to report people's words.
We said that we would go.
We promised that we would go.

1 Look at the table. Which verb do we use to report questions?

admit	deny	state
announce	explain	suggest
ask	promise	tell (somebody)
claim	report	think
confirm	say	

2 Choose the best option.

1 The advert **claimed** / **thought** that the product was better than all the others.
2 The shop assistant **told** / **asked** if I had bought the product before.
3 I **told** / **said** my mum that I wanted a bike.
4 My dad **reported** / **suggested** that I had spent too much money.

Tell has a different pattern to the other reporting verbs.
The teacher told us that we'd worked well.
The teacher said that we'd worked well.

3 Match the beginnings of the sentences (1–5) with the endings (a–e).

1 The bank told me that
2 The man admitted that
3 The newspaper reported that
4 The company announced that
5 The report confirmed that

a a spacecraft had landed on Mars.
b they were opening a new shop.
c he had made a mistake.
d the information was correct.
e there was no money in my account.

Working on your own

4 Choose four verbs from the table in Exercise 1. Write sentences reporting things people said last week.

word combinations with *money*

There are some verbs and expressions that we often use with *money*.
'You'll never win – you're wasting your money.'

1 Choose the correct option.

borrow	give	make
change	lend	raise
earn	lose	save

Joe: Can I (**1**) **borrow** / **make** some money?
Mum: I (**2**) **changed** / **gave** you some yesterday!
Joe: I know, but I've (**3**) **lost** / **spent** it.
Mum: Already? Well, I'm not going to (**4**) **lend** / **raise** you any more, sorry.

2 Match the questions (1–5) with the answers (a–e).

1 Do you ever borrow money?
2 How much money do you earn?
3 Have you ever won any money?
4 Do you waste a lot of money?
5 Do you save money every month?

a Nothing – I haven't got a job.
b Yes I do. I want to buy a new computer.
c Yes, every week from my dad.
d Yes, I buy lots of things I don't really need.
e No. I don't do the lottery or things like that.

3 Match the expressions (1–5) with the meanings (a–e).

1 I'm short of money.
2 I'm terrible with money.
3 It's a waste of money.
4 I'm good with money.
5 It's good value for money.

a I can't save. / I spend too much.
b I haven't got much at the moment.
c I save / spend wisely.
d It's a good product for the price.
e It's not a good product (for the price).

Working on your own

4 Write your own sentences to show the meaning of each combination.

lose money **make money** **raise money**

VIDEO WORKSHEET

1 The adventure capital of the world

New Zealand is a land of many beautiful and quiet natural places. Queenstown, on South Island, is beautiful, but it isn't quiet. People go to Queenstown looking for thrills and excitement. It is the adventure sports capital of the world. Bungee jumping actually began in Queenstown.

Before you watch

1 Read the introduction and discuss the questions.

1 Why do people visit Queenstown?
2 Which adventure sport is Queenstown particularly famous for?
3 What would you feel like if you did a bungee jump?

While you watch

PART ONE: Activities around Queenstown

2 Watch the first part of the film and choose the correct answer (a, b or c).

1 The bungee jump is about:
a 34 metres. **b** 134 metres. **c** 440 metres.
2 Jet boats were especially designed for New Zealand's:
a rivers. **b** lakes. **c** seas.
3 How do people in Queenstown feel about being 'the adventure capital of the world'?
a Important. **b** Excited. **c** Proud.

3 Complete the sentences (1–3) below.

1 Visitors to New Zealand can experience the New Zealand **l**............ .
2 The jet boats can work in **s**............ water.
3 Jet boats are also good at giving customers a **t**............ .

Watch again and check your answers.

PART TWO: In the mountains

4 Watch the second part of the film and choose the correct answer (a, b or c) for each question.

1 How do hikers get down from the mountain?
a They walk. **b** They fly. **c** They ski.
2 What do adventure sports in New Zealand help?
a Helicopter companies.
b Local culture.
c The tourism industry.
3 According to Van Asch, who has the best bungee jumping experience?
a People who have jumped many times.
b People who aren't frightened.
c People who have to try hard to jump.

5 Complete the sentences (1–3) below.

1 From the mountain, it's a five-minute **f**............ by helicopter back to the city.
2 The **b**............ of adventure tourism in New Zealand is the Kawarau Bridge.
3 The Kawarau Bridge was the world's first commercial bungee-jumping **s**............ .

Watch again and check your answers.

After you watch

6 Test your memory. How many of these options can you remember? Test your partner then watch the whole film.

1 The first bungee jumper feels **excited** / **ready**.
2 The jet boat driver makes the boat **jump over a rock** / **spin around**.
3 The tour guide says the hikers stay at the top of the mountain for **five hours** / **ten minutes**.
4 Marlene, the bungee jumper, **wants to jump again immediately** / **never wants to jump again**.

VIDEO WORKSHEET

2 Orangutan language

Orangutans are primates that come from Indonesia and Malaysia. They are highly intelligent animals, and in Malay their name actually means 'person of the forest' because they are so like humans. Orangutans can even communicate through language. At the National Zoo in Washington, D.C., two orangutans named Inda and Azie are part of a project with researcher Rob Shumaker.

Before you watch

1 **Read the introduction and discuss the questions.**

1 What does 'orangutan' mean in Malay?
2 Who are Inda and Azie?
3 What do you know about orangutans?

While you watch

PART ONE: The orangutan language project

2 **Watch the first part of the film and choose the correct answer (a, b or c) for each question.**

1 What is the aim of the project?
 a To teach the orangutans English.
 b To understand how orangutans behave in captivity.
 c To understand more about orangutan mental ability.
2 What is Inda learning?
 a How to use a computer.
 b A vocabulary of different symbols.
 c To communicate with visitors.
3 What can Inda do?
 a She can make sentences with symbols.
 b She can draw symbols of food.
 c She can find objects.

3 **Complete the sentences (1–3) below.**

1 Orangutans are highly developed **p**............s.
2 Apes in captivity need a **s**............ physical and mental environment.
3 The language programme is a **v**............ activity for the orangutans.

Watch again and check your answers.

PART TWO: Think tank

4 **Watch the second part of the film and choose the correct answer (a, b or c).**

1 Azie ... Inda.
 a is the same as
 b isn't as intelligent as
 c isn't as social as
2 The Think Tank exhibit at the zoo:
 a educates the public.
 b rescues wild orangutans.
 c is a behind-the-scenes activity.
3 According to Shumaker, why has the language project been successful?
 a Because he developed the symbols.
 b Because Inda and Azie enjoy it.
 c Because it's important.

5 **Complete the sentences (1–3) below.**

1 Each orangutan is an **i**............ .
2 Orangutans could become **e**............ in the wild in the next ten to twelve years.
3 Shumaker says the language project is a **t**............ **e**............ .

Watch again and check your answers.

After you watch

6 **Watch the whole film. Are the sentences true (T) or false (F)?**

1 At the National Zoo, the orangutans have lots of freedom to move around. **T / F**
2 Inda is sometimes quicker than the computer. **T / F**
3 All the orangutans in the language project show the same progress. **T / F**
4 Inda and Azie are sister and brother. **T / F**

VIDEO WORKSHEET

3 Dinosaur search

In the Sahara Desert there are so many dinosaur fossils buried under the sand that you could call it Africa's dinosaur graveyard. Palaeontologist Dr Paul Sereno and his team are looking for clues to find these dinosaur bones. Some of the bones have been hidden there for hundreds of millions of years. The team goes to Niger and makes an amazing discovery.

Before you watch

1 Read the introduction and discuss the questions.

1 Why is the Sahara desert 'Africa's dinosaur graveyard'?
2 How long have the bones been in the Sahara?
3 Do you know any other kinds of animals that have left fossils?

While you watch

PART ONE: Working in the Sahara desert

2 Watch the first part of the film and choose the correct answer (a, b or c) for each question.

1 Dr Sereno hasn't been back to the Sahara since 1997. Why not?
 a Because he didn't find any fossils in 1997.
 b Because it isn't easy to plan this kind of trip.
 c Because he was working on other fossils.
2 What happens when the team gets to Niger?
 a They find bones everywhere.
 b They don't find any bones.
 c The bones take a long time to find.
3 What problem does the team have?
 a They haven't got much water.
 b Their water truck doesn't arrive.
 c They spend a day and a half without water.

3 Complete the sentences (1–3) below.

1 The Sahara desert is a dinosaur **g**............ .
2 The **s**............ for dinosaur bones is led by Dr Sereno.
3 Dinosaurs were **p**............ animals.

Watch again and check your answers.

PART TWO: The discovery

4 Watch the second part of the film and choose the correct answer (a, b or c) for each question.

1 What is the team's biggest discovery?
 a A prehistoric crocodile leg.
 b A prehistoric crocodile pelvis.
 c A prehistoric crocodile jaw.
2 How was the 'super croc' different from today's crocodiles?
 a It was much bigger.
 b It was far smaller.
 c It was much older.
3 What do the experts know about the 'super croc'?
 a They know what it ate and how it hunted.
 b They don't know very much about it yet.
 c They know it lived in the desert.

5 Complete the sentences (1–3) below.

1 The team doesn't have to **w**............ about finding fossils.
2 The team carefully documents each **f**............ they make.
3 The team will find more information about the 'super croc' in the **s**............ .

Watch again and check your answers.

After you watch

6 Watch the whole film. Put the events (a–f) in the order in which they happened.

a Brady Barr visited the team.
b The palaeontology team found bones from lots of animals.
c The team almost ran out of water.
d Dr Sereno first found fossils in the Sahara.
e The team discovered part of a prehistoric crocodile.
f Dr Sereno took a team back to Niger.

VIDEO WORKSHEET

4 The Olympians

The modern Olympic Games are held every four years in a different country. The world's top athletes test their skills and determination in their sports. The Olympic Games began in ancient Greece as part of a festival which was dedicated to the Greek god Zeus. The event was a mix of athletic skill and religion. There was a long period when the games were not held. The modern games were brought back to life in Athens in 1896.

Before you watch

1 Read the introduction and discuss the questions.

1 What are the origins of the Olympic Games?

2 Why do we call today's games 'the modern Olympic Games'?

3 How many Olympic cities and Olympic events can you name?

While you watch

PART ONE: The athletes

2 Watch the first part of the film and choose the correct answer (a, b or c) for each question.

1 Where did the athletes in the ancient games come from?

a Greece. **b** Olympia.

c The ancient Greek world.

2 What were the rules for athletes in the ancient games?

a Athletes had to be under 30 years old.

b Athletes had to train for ten months.

c Athletes had to enter five different events.

3 Which event tested animal-hunting skills?

a The discus. **b** The long jump.

c The javelin.

3 Complete the sentences (1–3) below.

1 The Olympic Games represented the highest form of physical **a**............ .

2 Runners ran in front of a **c**............ of up to 40,000 people.

3 Long jumpers at the time used to hold **w**............**s** in their hands.

Watch again and check your answers.

PART TWO: The events

4 Watch the second part of the film and choose the correct answer (a, b or c) for each question.

1 Which sports took place in the Palaestra?

a Wrestling and boxing.

b Chariot racing and horse riding.

c Discus and long jump.

2 What were the categories in wrestling and boxing?

a Men and women. **b** Men and boys.

c Size and weight.

3 Why did Theodosius I stop the Olympics?

a Because he started new Roman games.

b Because he stopped all Greek festivals.

c Because they were related to ancient religious figures.

5 Complete the sentences (1–3) below.

1 Some Olympic events tested strength, others tested **s**............ .

2 Boxing matches in the ancient games had no **t**............ **l**............s.

3 The Olympic olive wreath was a sign of **d**............ .

Watch again and check your answers.

After you watch

6 Test your memory. How many of these questions can you answer? Test your partner then watch the whole film.

1 According to legend, who was Coroebus?

2 What were the five pentathlon sports?

3 Which events took place in the Hippodrome?

4 What did Olympic winners used to win?

5 There was a long period without the Olympics. How many years was this?

VIDEO WORKSHEET

5 Silk weavers of Vietnam

In China, the technique of making silk fabric from the cocoons of moths was kept secret for over 2,500 years. Then other countries learned how to produce silk. In the Vietnamese town of Vong Nguyet, village people keep and feed the moths and collect the cocoons. The silk fibres from the cocoons are made into thread. Then silk cloth is made by weaving the threads.

Before you watch

1 Read the introduction and discuss the questions.

1 Which country did silk come from originally?

2 Is silk a natural or an artificial fabric?

3 What are three stages in the life cycle of a silkworm moth?

While you watch

PART ONE: The silkworms

2 Watch the first part of the film and choose the correct answer (a, b or c).

1 Chinese royal families used to think that silk was worth more than:

a gold. **b** diamonds. **c** water.

2 How long do the silkworm caterpillars live for?

a Three days. **b** Three weeks. **c** Three months.

3 How long does it take a caterpillar to complete a cocoon?

a Three hours. **b** Three days. **c** Three weeks.

3 Complete the sentences (1–3) below.

1 The caterpillars eat only **m**............ **l**............ .

2 A silk **f**............ comes out of the caterpillar's head.

3 The farmers don't allow the caterpillar to become an **a**............ moth.

Watch again and check your answers.

PART TWO: Making the silk

4 Watch the second part of the film and choose the correct answer (a, b or c) for each question.

1 What is the first step in making the silk?

a Find a single thread. **b** Heat the cocoons. **c** Break the cocoons.

2 What are the modern spinning machines like?

a They give higher quality thread, but are slower.

b They give lower quality thread, but are faster.

c They give higher quality thread and are faster.

3 How much silk material can be made in two and a half hours?

a One metre. **b** Two metres. **c** Ten metres.

5 Complete the sentences (1–3) below.

1 When the cocoons are heated, the silk becomes **l**............ .

2 Silk cloth is made on machines called **l**............s.

3 The process of **w**............ the silk cloth is very slow.

Watch again and check your answers.

After you watch

6 Watch the whole film. Put the words and phrases in the correct order to make questions. Then answer the questions.

1 secret / by / taken away / was / which / a Chinese princess?

2 the caterpillars / placed / when / are / on tree trunks?

3 found / must / by / what / be / hand?

4 be / the silk thread / will / where / sent?

5 all of / must / what / watched / be / the time?

VIDEO WORKSHEET

6 Sleepy Hollow

American author Washington Irving wrote a well-known story about a town called Sleepy Hollow. The town is near New York City, in the Hudson River Valley. It was a quiet town of farmers when Irving visited it 200 years ago. Although the town has changed into a busy place, the people who live there still love and celebrate Irving's scary story, 'The Legend of Sleepy Hollow.'

Before you watch

1 Read the introduction and discuss the questions.

1. Where is Sleepy Hollow?
2. Why is it famous?
3. What do Sleepy Hollow residents think of the legend?

While you watch

PART ONE: The story

2 Watch the first part of the film and choose the correct answer (a, b or c) for each question.

1. Who was Ichabod Crane?
   - **a** A horseman with no head.
   - **b** An American writer.
   - **c** A teacher in the story.
2. Who were the old storytellers in the town of Sleepy Hollow?
   - **a** Farmers.
   - **b** Grandpas.
   - **c** Schoolmasters.
3. What happens in the story of Sleepy Hollow?
   - **a** The headless horseman hides in the church.
   - **b** The headless horseman falls off the bridge.
   - **c** The teacher races away from the headless horseman.

3 Complete the sentences (1–3) below.

1. **D**............ people came to live and farm in Sleepy Hollow in the 1600s.
2. Washington Irving visited the town when he was a **y**............ .
3. Katrina Van Tassel is a **c**............ in the story.

Watch again and check your answers.

PART TWO: The town

4 Watch the second part of the film and choose the correct answer (a, b or c) for each question.

1. How do the town's residents celebrate the story every year?
   - **a** They eat in 'The Horseman' restaurant.
   - **b** They light jack-o-lanterns in the dark.
   - **c** It's part of the Halloween festival.
2. When did Washington Irving live in the town?
   - **a** When he was writing the story.
   - **b** When he was a child.
   - **c** When he was an adult.
3. What happened when the trains came?
   - **a** A car factory was built.
   - **b** Washington Irving left.
   - **c** A factory closed.

5 Complete the sentences (1–3) below.

1. Carmen Cruz asks herself if the story is **r**............ or a legend.
2. A jack-o-lantern with a **c**............ in it can weigh 20 pounds.
3. There's a **c**............ of books written by Irving in his old house by the river.

Watch again and check your answers.

After you watch

6 Watch the whole film. Are the sentences true (T) or false (F) – or is there not enough information (N) to decide?

1. Sleepy Hollow is a real town. **T / F / N**
2. The headless horseman rode a horse called Gunpowder. **T / F / N**
3. Irving's house is open to visitors. **T / F / N**

VIDEO WORKSHEET

7 Wild animal town

Kariba is a town of 30,000 people in Zimbabwe. The town was built in a wildlife area, so elephants and other wild animals lived in the area first. While the town developed and grew, the people and animals got used to each other. Now they live side by side. Glenn Tatham lives in Kariba and he has worked with animals his whole life. He says that Kariba is unlike anywhere else on Earth.

Before you watch

1 Read the introduction and discuss the questions.

1. Where is Kariba?
2. What is unusual about Kariba?
3. What problems could there be in a town where both people and animals live?

While you watch

PART ONE: Kariba by day

2 Watch the first part of the film and choose the correct answer (a, b or c).

1. Buffaloes:
   - **a** are the most dangerous animals in Africa.
   - **b** are not at all dangerous.
   - **c** can be frightening at times.
2. The hippos in Kariba:
   - **a** are wild.
   - **b** are tame.
   - **c** have been captured.
3. Why was Kariba built originally?
   - **a** Because people wanted to live near animals.
   - **b** Because the river Zambezi was a good place to live.
   - **c** Because people working on the dam needed somewhere to live.

3 Complete the sentences (1–3) below.

1. Glenn Tatham used to be a **w**............ .
2. The town of Kariba was built **i**............ **t**............ **b**............ .
3. There is **t**............ between the people and the animals in Kariba.

Watch again and check your answers.

PART TWO: Kariba by night

4 Watch the second part of the film and choose the correct answer (a, b or c) for each question.

1. What happens at night in the town?
   - **a** The animals cause a lot of problems.
   - **b** The animals are attacked by dogs.
   - **c** The animals do what they want.
2. What happens in game corridors?
   - **a** Animals can move freely.
   - **b** People can drive freely.
   - **c** New developments are allowed.
3. According to Tatham, who has the right to stay in the town?
   - **a** The animals.
   - **b** The people.
   - **c** Both the animals and the people.

5 Complete the sentences (1–3) below.

1. There have been very few human **i**............ .
2. Tatham goes down to the lake after each day's **r**............ **h**............ .
3. In Kariba, there is a **b**............ between animals and people.

Watch again and check your answers.

After you watch

6 Watch the whole film and answer the questions.

1. Which animals can you see on the streets of Kariba?
2. Where was a dam built in the 1950s?
3. What are the 'rules' about life in Kariba?
4. What problems might affect the wild animals in the future?

VIDEO WORKSHEET

8 Madagascar perfume

The island of Madagascar is renowned for its distinctive wildlife, but some scientists visit the island for other reasons. A group of Swiss scientists is in Madagascar to investigate the island's smells and tastes. They are looking for new essences in plants and flowers.

Before you watch

1 Read the introduction and discuss the questions.

1 What is Madagascar famous for?
2 Where are essences found?
3 How are essences used?

While you watch

PART ONE: Looking for the essences

2 Watch the first part of the film and choose the correct answer (a, b or c) for each question.

1 Where exactly do the scientists go to look for new flowers?
 a To the river. b Along a forest path.
 c Into the tops of the trees.
2 What happens in the laboratory?
 a The scientists recreate the scents.
 b The scientists store the flowers.
 c The scientists analyse the essences.
3 Why is Professor Kaiser happy?
 a Because he found a new flower on the Tampolo River.
 b Because he's had a great experience in Madagascar.
 c Because he has recreated a very similar scent to the one he found.

3 Complete the sentences (1–3) below.

1 Vanilla and jasmine are two flower **s**............s.
2 The scientists get to the treetops by **b**............ .
3 The scents are used in a **v**............ of products.

Watch again and check your answers.

PART TWO: Using the essences

4 Watch the second part of the film and choose the correct answer (a, b or c).

1 The scientists have found some fruit:
 a whose taste is special.
 b whose taste is unknown.
 c whose smell is unusual.
2 What are the scientists' discoveries like?
 a Sometimes they're fantastic.
 b Sometimes they aren't new.
 c Sometimes they aren't very special.
3 What proportion of the new scents and flavours will be used in products?
 a Almost all of them. b Only a few of them.
 c About half of them.

5 Complete the sentences (1–3) below.

1 The scientists can use new fruit essences to make new **f**............**s**.
2 Willi Grab says the fruit tastes **j**............ and acidic.
3 The next time you **p**............ perfume, you could be smelling a scent from Madagascar.

Watch again and check your answers.

After you watch

6 Watch the whole film. Put the words and phrases in the correct order to make sentences. Then decide if the sentences are true (T) or false (F).

1 a flower. / discovered / claimed / a scientist / he
 .... **T / F**
2 reported that / technology / used / the narrator / the scientists / to recreate scents.
 .... **T / F**
3 he / on the Tampolo River. / had experienced / said that / the scent / Professor Kaiser
 .... **T / F**

Grammar Explorer

Unit 1

present simple, continuous and perfect

present simple

We use **present simple** to talk about:

- a regular activity, habit, activity often repeated
  I watch* The X Factor *every week.
- a permanent state
  My sister works in a department store.

We also use **present simple** to talk about:

- facts, general truths, laws of nature
  Pollution causes global warming.
- feelings and thoughts (see below: *verbs without a continuous form*)
  I hate TV soap operas.

Affirmative		
I/You/We/You/They He/She/It	make ... / watch ... / etc makes ... / watches ... / etc	
Negative		
I/You/We/You/They He/She/It	don't (do not) doesn't (does not)	make ... / watch ... / etc

Questions		
Do Does	I/you/we/you/they he/she/it	make ... / watch ... / etc?

Short answers					
Yes,	I/you/ we/you/they	do.	No,	I/you/ we/you/they	don't.
	he/she/it	does.		he/she/it	doesn't.

present continuous

We use the **present continuous** to talk about:

- an activity in progress – that is, which is happening now, at the time when we are talking
  Please be quiet – I'm watching my favourite TV show, and you're making so much noise I can't hear the singers!
- a temporary situation, around the time when we are talking
  He applied to be a contestant on a talent show, and he's waiting to hear if he's been accepted.

Affirmative		
I'm You're/We're/ You're/They're He's/She's/It's	(I am) (You/We/You/They are) (He/She/It is)	watching TV.
Negative		
I'm not You/We/You/They aren't He/She/It isn't	(I am not) (are not) (is not)	watching TV.

Questions		
Am Are Is	I you/we/you/they he/she/it	watching TV?

Short answers			
Yes,	I am. you/we/you/they are. he/she/it is.	No,	I'm not. you/we/you/they aren't. he/she/it isn't.

Notice the contrast between the present simple and the present continuous:

Present simple	
regular activity	permanent state
Present continuous	
activity in progress	temporary situation

verbs without a continuous form

Some verbs are called 'stative' or 'state' verbs, because they describe a state, feeling or thought rather than an action. We don't normally use present continuous with these verbs. They include:

believe, hate, know, like, love, need, prefer, seem, sound, think, understand, want

I love reality TV shows. (*Not: I ~~am loving~~ ...*)
That celebrity seems quite arrogant. (*Not: That celebrity ~~is seeming~~ ...*)
I think this show is a bit boring. (*Not: I ~~am thinking~~ ...*)
Many teenagers want to become famous through reality TV. (*Not: Many teenagers ~~are wanting~~ ...*)

present perfect

We use the **present perfect** to talk about:

- an action that happened during a period of time that started in the past and goes up to the present.
  (Exactly when the action happened is not known or not important.)
  I've watched this programme before.
  (an hour ago? a week ago? a year ago?)

- a state that began in the past, but continues up to the present.
  She has been a successful singer since she was a teenager.
  (She is still a successful singer now.)
- an action that has been completed a very short time ago. (This is almost always used with *just*.)
  They have just announced the winners of the competition.
  (They announced this a few seconds/minutes/etc ago.)
- an action that happened in the recent past, but which has a result in the present.
  (Notice that although we understand that the action happened in the past, we do not mention exactly when it happened.)
  He isn't on the show tonight because he's broken his leg.
  (Perhaps he broke it a few days ago, but we emphasise the result that this has tonight.)

<table>
<tr><th colspan="5">Affirmative</th></tr>
<tr><td colspan="2">I/You/We/You/They
He/She/It</td><td>'ve (have)
's (has)</td><td colspan="2">been ... / done ... / etc</td></tr>
<tr><th colspan="5">Negative</th></tr>
<tr><td colspan="2">I/You/We/You/They
He/She/It</td><td>haven't (have not)
hasn't (has not)</td><td colspan="2">been ... / done ... / etc</td></tr>
<tr><th colspan="5">Question</th></tr>
<tr><td>Have</td><td>I/you/ we/they</td><td colspan="3" rowspan="2">(ever) been ... / done ... / etc?</td></tr>
<tr><td>Has</td><td>he/she/it</td></tr>
<tr><th colspan="5">Short answers</th></tr>
<tr><td rowspan="2">Yes,</td><td>I/you/we/they have.</td><td rowspan="2">No,</td><td>I/you/we/they</td><td>haven't.</td></tr>
<tr><td>he/she/it has.</td><td>he/she/it</td><td>hasn't.</td></tr>
</table>

present perfect and past simple

We have seen that we use the **present perfect** to talk about something happening in the past, as long as the action or time period has some connection with the present.

However, we do not use the present perfect to talk about completed action at a finished time in the past – we use the **past simple** instead.

We use this when:

- we say or understand when the action happened
  My favourite contestant left the show last week.
- we know that the period of time in which it happened is completely in the past and does not continue up to the present
  Charles Dickens wrote more than a dozen famous novels.
  (He died in 1870.)

present perfect with ever and never

We can use the words ***ever*** and ***never*** with the present perfect to refer to **experiences** – that is, something which someone has/hasn't done, at any time in their whole life up to the present.

We use ***ever*** in present perfect questions.
Ever always goes before the main verb.
Have you ever been on TV?

We use ***never*** in negative sentences with the present perfect.
Never always goes before the main verb.
I've never met a rock star.

present perfect with It's the first time ...

We can also use ***It's the first/second/etc time ...*** with the present perfect to talk about experiences.
This expression is mainly used in affirmative sentences.
We begin the sentence with *It's the first time*, followed by subject + verb in the present perfect.
In informal spoken English, we often add the word *ever* for emphasis. ***It's the first time I've (ever) spoken to a TV celebrity.***

present perfect with for and since

We use the word ***for*** with the present perfect to talk about *duration* – that is, how long it has been from the start of a state or situation until now.
For is followed by a phrase that describes a period of time.
She has been a singer for three years.

We use the word ***since*** with the present perfect, for a state or situation which has continued up to the present, to talk about when it started.
Since is followed by a time/day/year/etc, or a phrase that describes a particular time.
She has been a singer since 2007.
I have loved cartoons since I was a young child.

yet, still, already and *just*

yet

We use the word ***yet*** with the **present perfect** in questions and negative sentences.
Yet with the present perfect always goes at the end of the sentence or clause.
We use *yet* to suggest that if something has not already happened, we expect it will happen soon.
Have you seen the new reality show yet?
No, I haven't seen it yet. I'll watch it this evening, though.

Grammar Explorer

We can also use ***yet*** with the **present simple** in questions and negative sentences.
As with the present perfect, *yet* with the present simple always goes at the end of the sentence or clause.
Is it time for the show to start yet?
No, it isn't time yet. It starts after the news.

still

We use the word ***still*** with the **present perfect** in negative sentences.
Still with the present perfect always goes immediately before *haven't/hasn't*.
We use *still* to show that something has not happened/changed yet; it often suggests that someone would expect the action/situation/etc to have happened/changed by now.
***I still haven't decided who to vote for on* The X Factor.**

We can also use ***still*** with the **present simple** and **present continuous** in questions and affirmative sentences.
Still with the present simple goes before the main verb, but after the verb *be*.
I'm a teenager now, but I still like watching some children's TV shows.
He didn't sing very well on last night's show, but he's still my favourite contestant.
Still with the present continuous goes between the auxiliary *be* and the main verb in *-ing*.
I'm going to be a bit late, I'm afraid – I'm still trying to decide what to wear.

We can also use ***still*** with the **present simple** and **present continuous** in negative sentences, but this is not very common.
I've listened to this song several times, but I still don't understand what it's about.

already

We use the word ***already*** with the **present perfect** in affirmative sentences.
Already with the present perfect usually goes between *have/has* and the main verb.
We often use *already* to suggest that something has happened sooner than we expected.
She's only 19, but she has already starred in a popular comedy series on TV.

We can also use ***already*** with the **present simple** in affirmative sentences.
Already with the present simple usually goes before the main verb, but after the verb *be*.
The show only started a week ago, but I already know which contestant I like best.
The new show is already very popular.

just

We usually use the word ***just*** with the **present perfect** in affirmative sentences.
Just with the present perfect always goes between *have/has* and the main verb.
We use *just* to show that something has happened a (very) short time ago.
A new soap opera has just started on this channel. I watched the first episode last night.

because and because of

Because and ***because of*** are both used to introduce the reason for the action, state, opinion, etc which is mentioned in the main part of the sentence.
Because (of), followed by the reason, comes after the main part of the sentence.

Because is followed by a clause – that is, subject + full verb.
This soap opera is popular because it deals with real-life situations.
She's my favourite singer because she's got such an unusual voice.

Because of is followed by a noun or noun phrase.
Filming the outdoor scenes for the series was delayed because of rain.
This show isn't suitable for children, because of all the violence and bad language.

Notice that in written English, *because* and *because of* join the state, opinion, etc and the reason into one sentence.
In informal spoken English, the state, opinion, etc may be mentioned in the speaker's previous sentence, and the reason may be given in a separate (grammatically incomplete) sentence.
A: I really like this comedy series.
B: Do you? Why?
A: Because it's so funny!

Unit 2

present perfect continuous

We use the **present perfect continuous** to talk about a continuous activity which began in the past and has continued up to the present.

A 'continuous activity' is a single activity, rather than a series of actions, which was in progress all the time.
'Has continued up to the present' means that the activity is still in progress now (or has just finished).

present perfect simple				
have/has	+	past participle		
present continuous				
		be	+	present participle
present perfect continuous				
have/has	+	*been*	+	*-ing*

We form the present perfect continuous with ***have been*** or ***has been***, followed by the **present participle** of the main verb.
We form the negative with ***haven't been*** or ***hasn't been***, followed by the present participle of the main verb.
We make present perfect continuous questions by putting ***Have/Has*** before the subject, and then ***been***, followed by the present participle of the main verb.
In short answers we use ***have/has*** or ***haven't/hasn't***. We DON'T use ***been*** or the main verb.

Affirmative			
I/You/We/You/They He/She/It	've (have) 's (has)	been	studying / etc
Negative			
I/You/We/You/They He/She/It	haven't (have not) hasn't (has not)	been	studying / etc

Question			
Have Has	I/you/ we/they he/she/it	been	studying / etc?

Short answers					
Yes,	I/you/ we/they he/she/it	have. has.	No,	he/she/it I/you/ we/they	haven't. hasn't.

present perfect continuous with for and since

We use the word ***for*** with the present perfect continuous to talk about *duration* – that is, how long it has been from the start of a continuous activity until now.
For is followed by a phrase that describes a period of time.
I've been studying English for four years.

We use the word ***since*** with the present perfect continuous, for an activity which has continued up to the present, to talk about when it started.
Since is followed by a time/day/year/etc, or a phrase that describes a particular time.
I've been studying English since 2007.
since the age of twelve.

present perfect continuous and present perfect simple

We have seen that we use the **present perfect continuous** to talk about a continuous activity beginning in the past and continuing up to the present.
I've been sending emails all morning.
(We see this as one activity.)

However, we use the **present perfect simple** – not the present perfect continuous – to talk about:

- a series of completed actions beginning in the past and continuing up to the present
  I've sent fifteen emails so far this morning.
  (By emphasising the number, we present this as fifteen separate actions.)
- a single decision, conclusion, etc which is the result of the continuous activity
  I've already received several replies.
- a state, thought or feeling, beginning in the past and continuing up to the present; see Unit 1: *verbs without a continuous form*
  I've been reading this book for over an hour, but I haven't understood *(not 'haven't been understanding')* ***what it's about.***

relative clauses

We can join two short sentences together by making the second sentence into a **relative clause**; the first sentence contains the main information, and the relative clause gives further information about this.

The relative clause contains a pronoun or adverb which relates to a noun in the first sentence.
A bonobo is a very intelligent animal. *(main information)*
It is a type of chimpanzee. *(further information)*
(The pronoun 'it' relates to the noun 'bonobo'.)

We join the two parts of the sentence by changing the pronoun into a **relative pronoun** (e.g. *which*) and putting it next to the noun it relates to, followed by the rest of the relative clause.
(Notice that the relative pronoun REPLACES the subject pronoun – we DON'T use both pronouns together.)
A bonobo, which is a type of chimpanzee, is a very intelligent animal. (Not: which ~~it~~ is a type ...)

defining and non-defining relative clauses

The meaning of the first sentence is sometimes incomplete without the further information given in the relative clause. The relative clause defines the noun in the first sentence, and so it is a **defining relative clause**.
People are afraid of heights. *(Which people? All people? Some people? The meaning of the sentence is not complete.)*
They have acrophobia. *(This defines which people we mean.)*
People who have acrophobia are afraid of heights.

The animals are chimpanzees. *(Which animals? The meaning of the sentence is not complete.)*
They are closest to humans. *(This defines which animals we mean.)*
The animals which are closest to humans are chimpanzees.

If the meaning of the first sentence is complete on its own, the relative clause doesn't define the noun in the first sentence – it simply gives extra information – and so it is a **non-defining relative clause**.
Crows can make their own tools. *(The meaning of the sentence is complete.)*
They are the most intelligent birds. *(This gives extra information.)*
Crows, which are the most intelligent birds, can make their own tools.

Grammar Explorer

Notice that a **defining relative clause** becomes part of the meaning of the main sentence, and so we DON'T use commas to separate the relative clause and the rest of the sentence.
People who have acrophobia are afraid of heights.
The animals which are closest to humans are chimpanzees.

With a **non-defining relative clause**, we DO use commas, before and after the relative clause, to separate the extra information from the main part of the sentence.
A bonobo, which is a type of chimpanzee, is a very intelligent animal.
Crows, which are the most intelligent birds, can make their own tools.

relative pronouns and relative adverbs

We have seen forming a relative clause involves replacing a pronoun or adverb with a relative pronoun or relative adverb. The **relative pronouns** we use are ***who***, ***which*** and ***whose***. The ***relative adverbs*** we use are ***when*** and ***where***.

For **people**, we use the relative pronoun ***who*** to replace the pronouns ***he, she, they, etc***.
People are afraid of heights. They have acrophobia.
People who have acrophobia are afraid of heights.

For **animals/things**, we use the relative pronoun ***which*** to replace the pronouns ***it, they, etc***.
A bonobo is a very intelligent animal. It is a type of chimpanzee.
A bonobo, which is a type of chimpanzee, is a very intelligent animal.

For **people** and **animals/things**, we use the relative pronoun ***whose*** to replace the pronouns ***his, her, their, its, etc***.
Derren Brown is a famous hypnotist. His TV show is very popular.
Derren Brown, whose TV show is very popular, is a famous hypnotist.

The bird couldn't fly. Its wing was broken.
The bird whose wing was broken couldn't fly.

For **times**, we use the relative adverb ***when*** to replace the adverb ***then***.
At eight o'clock there is a lot of traffic. Most people are going to work then.
At eight o'clock, when most people are going to work, there is a lot of traffic. *(Notice that 'then' goes next to 'eight o'clock', followed by the rest of the relative clause)*

For **places**, we use the relative adverb ***where*** to replace the adverb ***there***.
The place is a laboratory. Scientists do experiments there.
The place where scientists do experiments is a laboratory.
(Notice that 'where' goes next to 'place', followed by the rest of the relative clause)

In **defining** relative clauses – but not in non-defining relative clauses – we can use ***that*** instead of *who* or *which*.

People who have acrophobia are afraid of heights.
People that have acrophobia are afraid of heights.

The animals which are closest to humans are chimpanzees.
The animals that are closest to humans are chimpanzees.

question tags

Question tags are short questions added to the end of a statement. We use them mainly in spoken English. Question tags show that:

- the speaker expects/invites the listener(s) to say that they agree with the statement.
  My dog is lovely, (statement) ***isn't he?*** (question tag)
  – the speaker expects the answer 'Yes, he is.'
  You don't mind, (statement) ***do you?*** (question tag)
  – the speaker expects the answer 'No, I don't.'
- the speaker is not completely sure that the statement is correct, and wants to check.
  You're joking, (statement) ***aren't you?*** (question tag)
  – the speaker is not completely sure and wants to check.

We form a question tag with the same modal, auxiliary or form of *be* which is used in the statement, followed by the appropriate subject pronoun.
We do not use a name or a noun phrase in the question tag.
Joe will do the introduction, won't he? (Not: 'won't ~~Joe~~')
That dog is really smart, isn't it? (Not: 'isn't ~~that dog~~')

The question tag is the opposite of the statement – that is, if the statement is affirmative, the question tag is negative, and if the statement is negative, the question tag is affirmative.
Holly is (affirmative) ***very organised, isn't*** (negative) ***she?***
Joe hasn't (negative) ***got a good memory, has*** (affirmative) ***he?***

If there is no modal, auxiliary or form of *be* in the statement, we use ***don't/doesn't***.
You know what to do, don't you?
Joe keeps forgetting things, doesn't he?

Unit 3

past perfect

We have seen that we use the present perfect to talk about an action/event that happened at some time before the present.

In the same way, we use past perfect to talk about an action/event that happened at some time before another action, event or time in the past. Exactly when the earlier action/event happened is usually not known or is not important.
When I arrived at the station, the train had already left.
(It left at some time – 1 minute? 5 minutes? – before I arrived.)
By six o'clock the sun had set.
(It set at some time – 5.30? 5.45? 5.59? – before six o'clock.)

We don't have to present the two actions/events in the same order in which they happened, but we must use the past perfect for the one which happened first.
Dinosaurs had been extinct for millions of years by the time the first humans evolved.

By the time the first humans evolved, dinosaurs had been extinct for millions of years.

We form the past perfect with ***had/hadn't* + past participle** of the main verb. It has the same form for all subjects *(I, he, we, etc)*.
We form questions in the past perfect by putting ***Had*** before the subject, followed by the **past participle** of the main verb.

Affirmative		
I/You/He/She/ It/We/You/They	had	been ... / made ... / etc
Negative		
I/You/He/She/ It/We/You/They	hadn't (had not)	been ... / made ... / etc
Questions		
Had	I/you/he/she/it/we/you/they	been ... / made ... / etc ?
Short answers		
Yes, No,	I/you/he/she/it/we/you/they	had. hadn't.

used to

We can use ***used to*** for:

- past habits, states, etc. that are now finished
  I used to play with toy cars when I was a little boy. *(I don't now)*
  People used to believe the Moon was made of cheese. *(now we know it isn't)*
- things that existed or often happened in the past but do not exist/happen now.
  There used to be a farm here. *(now there's a shopping mall)*

The form is ***used to* + bare infinitive** of the main verb. It has the same form for all subjects *(I, you, he, etc)*.

We form the negative with ***didn't* + *use to* + bare infinitive** of the main verb. Again, the form is the same for all subjects *(I, you, he, etc)*.
People didn't use to have electricity in their homes. *(now they do)*

We form questions with ***Did* + subject + *use to* + bare infinitive** of the main verb.
Did you use to live in Manchester? *(you live London now)*

result clauses

Result clauses are used in sentences which first describe a situation and then say what happened/happens/will happen/ etc as a result of this situation.
The result clause joins the situation and the result in a single sentence.

Situation	**Result**
The food was very salty.	*I couldn't eat it.*

The food was so salty that I couldn't eat it.

We form result clauses with ***so* + adjective + *that* ...** or ***such (a/an)* + adjective + noun + *that* ...** . (Remember that with uncountable nouns we don't use *a/an*.)

The food was very salty. (adjective)
The food was so salty that I couldn't eat it.

It was a very salty meal. (adjective + countable noun)
It was such a salty meal that I couldn't eat it.
It was very salty food. (adjective + uncountable noun)
It was such salty food that I couldn't eat it.

We can also form result clauses with ***so many* + plural noun** or ***so much* + uncountable noun**.
There were so many people *(plural)* ***at the restaurant that we couldn't get a table.***
I ate so much food *(uncountable)* ***that afterwards I felt ill.***

Unit 4

tenses used for the future

The basic tense we use to talk about the future is the **future simple** – but this is not the only tense we use. We use a variety of tenses to talk about:

- **future plans and arrangements**
- **predictions**
- **promises, offers, etc**

future plans and arrangements

Will is only ONE of the tenses we use to talk about the future. When we talk about future plans and arrangements, we can use ***will***, ***going to***, **present continuous** and **present simple**. Each of these shows something slightly different about the plans/arrangements.

- ***will*** is used to talk about **'on-the-spot' decisions** – that is, decisions we make at the moment of speaking, usually about the near future. It is just a general decision – we have not yet made any plans or arrangements.
  I'm hungry – I think I'll make myself a sandwich.

- ***going to*** is used to talk about **plans** for the near future, but **without definite arrangements** (or without mentioning these); after thinking about it, we know what we want to do and we will arrange the details later.
  I'm going to do all my homework on Friday evening so I'll have the rest of the weekend free.

As well as for informal plans about the near future, we use ***going to*** for our **ambitions** in the more distant future.
I'm going to go to art college next year. I'm going to study graphic design.

- the **present continuous** is used to talk about **definite arrangements** for the near future; we know (and usually mention) final details such as day/date, time and place.
  I'm flying to Prague tomorrow on the ten o'clock flight from Heathrow.

Grammar Explorer

- **present simple** is used to talk about **'timetable'** arrangements which someone else makes, such as timetables for buses and trains, airline flight schedules, cinema times, the starting time of football matches, etc.
  The film starts at eight o'clock, so I'll meet you outside the cinema at half past seven.

predictions

- We can use ***will***, ***may*** and ***might*** for predictions about the future, based on what we think, believe or hope.
  One day we will probably send astronauts to Mars.
- We can use ***going to*** for predictions about the future, based on what we see or know – that is, based on some evidence in the present.
  Look at those big black clouds! It's going to rain.
- We can also use **future continuous** for predictions – see *future continuous*, below.

Will, ***may*** and ***might*** have the same form for all subjects *(I, you, he, etc)*. The main verb after these modals is in the **bare infinitive**.
The negative of ***will*** is ***won't*** *(will not)* and it is the same for all subjects. The negative of ***may*** and ***might*** is ***may not*** and ***might not***, and these are also the same for all subjects.

Using ***may*** instead of ***will*** often suggests we are not so sure about our prediction, and ***might*** usually suggests we are even less sure. We often use these modals after *I think*, *I'm sure*, etc, and/or with words such as *probably*, *perhaps*, *certainly*, etc, to show more clearly how sure we are about our prediction.
I'm sure I will find a career in design when I leave school.
I think I may work as a graphic designer.
Perhaps I might even become a fashion designer.

other uses of *will*

In addition to future plans and arrangements and predictions, *will* is used for:

- **offers**
  I'll help you with your homework if you like
- **promises**
  Can I borrow this CD? I promise I won't lose it.
- **warnings**
  If you do that again I'll be angry.
- **requests**
  Will you water my plants while I'm on holiday, please?
- **statements of fact about the future**
  It's my Mum's birthday next week. She'll be 45.

future continuous

The **future continuous** is used for actions that (we expect or predict) will be in progress at a specific time in the future.
At this time tomorrow, I'll be lying on the beach.
I can't meet you at six o'clock, because I'll be doing my homework.
People will be using much more solar power in twenty years' time.

We form the future continuous with ***will/won't + be + -ing***. It has the same form for all subjects *(I, he, we, etc)*.
We form questions in the future continuous by putting ***Will*** before the subject, and then ***be***, followed by the ***-ing*** form of the main verb.

Affirmative			
I/You/He/She/It/ We/You/They	'll (will)	be	doing ... / going ... / etc
Negative			
I/You/He/She/It/ We/You/They	won't (will not)	be	doing ... / going ... / etc
Questions			
Will	I/you/he/she/it/we/ you/they	be	doing ... / going ... / etc ?
Short answers			
Yes, No,	I/you/he/she/it/we/ you/they	will. won't.	

time expressions used for the future

Time expressions such as ***after***, ***as soon as***, ***before***, ***by the time***, ***when***, ***while*** and ***until*** can be used to talk about the future, but they are not followed by *will* – instead, they are followed by a present tense (usually the present simple).

- ***after***, ***before*** – used to show a sequence of actions/events
  I'll get dressed after I have a shower.
  (Not: after I ~~will~~ have)
  Finish your homework before you watch TV.
  (Not: before you ~~will~~ watch)
- ***as soon as*** – emphasises 'immediately after this'
  I'll go to bed as soon as I get home.
  (Not: as soon as I ~~will~~ get)
- ***by the time*** – means 'at some time before this'
  It'll be midnight by the time we finish.
  (Not: by the time we ~~will~~ finish)
- ***when*** – means 'at this time'
  Send me an email when you know what your plans are.
  (Not: when you ~~will~~ know)
- ***while*** – used for two things happening at the same time; mainly used with continuous tenses
  I'll be sitting at home while my friends are having a great time at the party. *(Not: while my friends ~~will be~~ having)*
- ***until*** – shows that something will change/happen after this, but not before
  Please remain seated until the exam is over.
  (Not: until the exam ~~will be~~)

Unit 5

the passive: present simple, past simple, present continuous, past continuous, present perfect

In active voice, the subject of the sentence is the person/thing/etc that does the action. When we use the **passive**, the subject is the person/thing/etc that the action happens to.

In other words, the object of a sentence in active voice becomes the subject of the sentence in the passive. If we want to say who/what does the action (the 'agent') in the passive, we use *by*.

SUBJECT	*VERB*	*OBJECT*	
The Ancient Greeks	***built***	***the Parthenon.***	(Active)
The Parthenon	***was built***	***by the Ancient Greeks.***	(Passive)
SUBJECT	*VERB*	*AGENT*	

We use the passive when we want to emphasise the subject and/or the action itself. If it is not important or not clear who/what the agent is (e.g. *someone*, *they*, *people*, etc), then we don't include it.

They have discovered the remains of a Roman settlement.
= The remains of a Roman settlement have been discovered ~~by them~~.

tenses in the passive

We form the passive with ***be*** + the **past participle** of the verb which is used in the active sentence; the tense of *be* is the same as the tense of the verb in the active sentence.

Simple tenses			
present	*is / are*		+ past participle
past	*was / were*		+ past participle
Continuous tenses			
present	*is / are*	*being*	+ past participle
past	*was / were*	*being*	+ past participle
Present perfect			
	has / have	*been*	+ past participle

Thousands of tourists visit the city every day. *(present simple)*
= The city is visited by thousands of tourists every day.

Volcanic ash covered Pompeii. *(past simple)*
= Pompeii was covered by volcanic ash.

Tourism is destroying the local culture. *(present continuous)*
= The local culture is being destroyed by tourism.

They were taking the treasure to Spain. *(past continuous)*
= The treasure was being taken to Spain ~~by them~~.

They have restored many of the old buildings. *(present perfect)*
= Many of the old buildings have been restored ~~by them~~.

the negative form of the passive

We form the negative by adding *n't* to the first modal/auxiliary in the sentence – that is, ***isn't/aren't*** in the present simple/continuous, ***wasn't/weren't*** in the past simple/continuous, and ***hasn't/haven't*** in the present perfect.

Damage to the monument isn't caused by the weather, but by tourists.
The building wasn't being used until they turned it into a museum.
A solution to the problem hasn't been found yet.

questions in the passive

We form questions in the passive by putting the first modal/auxiliary in the sentence – ***Is/Are***, ***Was/Were*** or ***Has/Have*** – before the subject.

Were famous places always protected by special laws?
Is the statue being displayed to the public?
Has anything been discovered about the people who lived here?

We can also begin questions with **question words** such as ***What***, ***Why***, ***Where***, ***How*** etc to ask for extra information rather than a simple 'Yes' or 'No' answer.

What is the statue made of?
Why has the ancient city been closed to tourists?
How were the Pyramids built?

the passive with modal verbs

We have seen that we form the passive with ***be*** + **past participle**, and that the tense/form of *be* is the same as the tense/form of the verb in the active sentence.

If a sentence in active voice contains a modal such as ***can/can't***, ***must/mustn't*** or ***will/won't***, the modal is followed by the **bare infinitive**.
In the same way, if a sentence in the passive contains one of these modals, the modal is followed by the bare infinitive of ***be***, and then the past participle of the main verb.

They can make beautiful jewellery from gold.
Beautiful jewellery can be made from gold.

People must do something about the problem.
Something must be done about the problem.

causative form

We use the **causative form** to talk about an action which the subject does not do themselves.
That is, someone else does the action for them (for example, cuts their hair, fixes their computer, etc), but the subject has the result of the action (a new haircut, a computer that works properly, etc).

Grammar Explorer

The causative form is ***have* + object + past participle** of the main verb.
Have is used as a normal verb in any tense.
I have my teeth checked every six months. (the dentist checks them)
Sandra had her car repaired yesterday. (a mechanic repaired it)
They're going to have the house painted. (painters are going to paint it)
Len has had his hair dyed blonde. (the hairdresser has dyed it)

As with the passive, we don't mention the agent (that is, the person who actually does the action) if it is obvious, not important or not clear.
She's having her hair cut this afternoon ~~by the hairdresser~~.

We can also use ***get* + object + past participle**, especially with tenses for the future, to emphasise that we will make arrangements for someone else to do something for us, or tell someone else to do it.

Unit 6

modal verbs for speculation

Speculation is guessing – that is, trying to decide, based on incomplete evidence, whether a suggested explanation, theory, etc is possible, impossible or probable.

We use the modal verbs ***may***, ***might***, ***could***, ***can't***, ***couldn't*** and ***must*** to speculate about an event or situation.
May, ***might*** and ***could*** all show that we think the explanation is possible; ***can't*** and ***couldn't*** show that we think this is impossible; and ***must*** shows that we think this is probable or perhaps almost certain.
Notice that we do not normally use ***can*** to speculate, and we NEVER use ***mustn't***; we normally use ***couldn't*** only for speculation about the past.

When we speculate about the present, the modals are followed by a normal **bare infinitive**.

(Situation: I don't know where my keys are)
They may / might / could be in my school bag, I suppose. *(it's possible)*
They can't be in my purse – I've looked there. *(it's impossible)*
They must be in the pocket of my other jeans – I think that's where I left them. *(it's probable)*

When we speculate about the past, the modals are followed by a bare **perfect infinitive** – that is, ***have* + past participle** of the main verb.

(Situation: I don't know why my friend didn't call me last night)
She may / might / could have fallen asleep, I suppose. *(it's possible)*
She can't / couldn't have forgotten – she always calls me. *(it's impossible)*
She must have lost her mobile again. *(it's probable)*

second conditional

We use the **second conditional** to talk about an imaginary action, situation or result which depends on an imaginary condition – *not* a real condition – in the present and/or future.

Do I have a good voice?
→ Real → No, I don't.
→ Imaginary → Yes, I do. → I'll become a rock star.

If I had a good voice, I'd become a rock star.

We form the second conditional with ***If* + past simple** for the condition, followed by ***would /wouldn't* * + bare infinitive** for the resulting action or situation. We do not use ***would*** for the condition.

*We can also use *could/couldn't* or *might/mightn't*, but this is the most common pattern.

We can put the two parts of the sentence in any order – but notice that when the sentence begins with the condition, we must put a comma between the condition and the result.
If I knew the answer (condition)**,** ***I'd tell you*** (result).
I would live in a big house (result) ***if I had lots of money*** (condition)**.**

> Notice that the use of past simple in the condition does not show completed action – it shows 'not real'.
> ***If* + past simple** = imaginary ('unreal'), in the present/future.

Unit 7

third conditional

We use the **third conditional** to talk about an imaginary action, event or situation in the past, which depends on an imaginary past condition.
The imaginary condition and the resulting action or situation are the opposite of what really happened.

> **What really happened:** *He didn't take a map, so he got lost.*
> **Imaginary situation:** *He took a map, so he didn't get lost.*
> ***If he had taken a map, he wouldn't have got lost.***

We form the third conditional with ***If* + past perfect** for the condition, followed by ***would/wouldn't* * + *have* + past participle** for the resulting action or situation.

*We can also use *could/couldn't* or *might/mightn't*, but this is the most common pattern.

We can put the two parts of the sentence in any order – but notice that when the sentence begins with the condition, we must put a comma between the condition and the result.
If we had been more careful (condition)***, the accident wouldn't have happened*** (result)**.**
I wouldn't have missed my train (result) ***if I had got up early*** (condition)**.**

could/should have done

We use ***could(n't) have / should(n't) have* + past participle** to talk about events, actions and situations in the past; we usually imagine something which is in contrast to what really happened.

could(n't) have

We use ***could(n't) have* + past participle** to talk about:

- **possibility**
  Why did you do that? You could have had an accident! *(This was a possibility – but it didn't happen.)*
- **ability / opportunity**
  Why didn't you tell me about your problem? I could have helped you. *(I had the ability to help you – but I didn't know, so I didn't help.)*
  Che Guevara could have become rich. *(He had the ability and/or opportunity to do this – but he decided not to.)*
  Don't feel bad - you couldn't have prevented what happened. *(Even if you had tried harder / in a different way, it wouldn't have worked.)*

should(n't) have

We use ***should(n't) have* + past participle** to talk about right and wrong. This includes:

- **results**
  Our team should have won the match – we were much better than them. *(This would have been the 'right' result – but it didn't happen.)*
- **regrets / criticism**
  I should have studied harder for the exam. *(This would have been the right thing to do – but I didn't do it.)*
  You shouldn't have shouted at her. *(You did shout at her – but it was the wrong thing to do.)*

regrets and criticism

Regrets are the feelings we have when we realise that we have made a bad decision in the past – that is, we did something that was wrong, or didn't do the right thing.

Criticism is when we tell someone else that they did something that was wrong, or didn't do the right thing.

I wish and *If only ... !*

We use ***I wish*** and ***If only ... !*** to make statements about imaginary situations which are the opposite of what really happened; they show that we regret what really happened.

When we talk about the past, *I wish* and *If only* are followed by the past perfect.

I stayed up late last night. (what really happened)
I wish / If only I hadn't stayed up late last night!

I didn't do my homework yesterday. (what really happened)
I wish / If only I'd done my homework yesterday!

We can use ***I wish ... !*** in the same way to criticise what someone else did or didn't do.

You told everyone my secret. (what really happened)
I wish you hadn't told everyone my secret!

You weren't honest about this. (what really happened)
I wish you'd been honest about this!

should(n't) have

We can also use ***should(n't) have* + past participle** to express our regrets or to criticise someone else's actions in the past.

I didn't think about it carefully. (what really happened)
I should have thought about it carefully.

I left it until the last minute. (what really happened)
I shouldn't have left it until the last minute.

You didn't listen to me. (what really happened)
You should have listened to me.

Unit 8

reported statements

direct and reported speech

Direct speech gives the exact words someone said and uses quotation marks ('...') to show this.
Reported speech gives the meaning of what somebody said, but doesn't use all their exact words and doesn't use quotation marks. For example, we use reported speech when we tell somebody else what another person said.
'I'll meet you here tomorrow,' John said to Susan. *(Direct speech)*
John said he would meet Susan there the next day. *(Reported speech)*

backshift

When we report what a person said, the time of speaking is not the same as the time of reporting. For example, what was the present at the time of speaking has usually already become the past at the time of reporting.

Grammar Explorer

For this reason, we often use 'backshift' in reported speech – that is, the tense of a verb used in direct speech moves one step back into the past.

Direct Speech	Reported Speech
Present Simple ***'We are very happy with the product.'***	Past Simple ***He said they were very happy with the product.***
Present Continuous ***'We are trying to make the product even better.'***	Past Continuous ***He said they were trying to make the product even better.***
Present Perfect ***'We have made several changes this year.'***	Past Perfect* ***He said they had made several changes that year.***
Past Simple ***'We made several changes last year, too.'***	Past Perfect* ***He said they had made several changes the year before, too.***
Present Perfect Continuous ***'We have been making the product for 10 years.'***	Past Perfect Continuous* ***He said they had been making the product for 10 years.***
Past Continuous ***'We were making the product 10 years ago.'***	Past Perfect Continuous* ***He said they had been making the product 10 years before.***
will ***'Customers will notice a big difference.'***	*would* ***He said customers would notice a big difference.***
can ***'Customers can order products online.'***	*could* ***He said customers could order products online.***
must / have to ***'We must keep our customers satisfied.'***	*had to* ***He said they had to keep their customers satisfied.***

** Notice that present perfect and past simple both 'backshift' to the same tense – past perfect. Present perfect continuous and past continuous both 'backshift' to past perfect continuous.*

other changes in reported speech

When we report what a person says, the place, listener(s), etc at the time of speaking are often different to the place, listener(s), etc at the time of reporting.
For example, imagine that on Monday John speaks to Susan in the park: - ***'I'll meet you here tomorrow,' John said.***
On Friday, Susan is in the cafeteria, telling a friend about the conversation; what was 'tomorrow' when John spoke is now several days ago, what was 'here' is now far away, and so on.
What Susan reports is: - ***John said he would meet me there the next day.***

Direct Speech	Reported Speech
I – we	he/she – they
me – us	him/her – them
my – your – our	his/her – their
here	there
this – these	that – those
now	then / at that time
last night/week/etc	the night/week/etc before / the previous night/week/etc
this morning/afternoon/etc	that morning/afternoon/etc
next week/July/etc	the next week/July/etc / the following week/July/etc
yesterday	the day before / the previous day
today	that day / the same day
tomorrow	the next/following day

reporting verbs

In direct speech, the exact words someone uses can show us if they are speaking (e.g.) politely, angrily, etc; in reported speech, where we don't use their exact words, we can use different **reporting verbs** to show this sort of information.

Direct speech	**Reported speech**
'Sit down – now!' he shouted.	***He ordered me to sit down.***
'Sit down,' he said	***He told me to sit down.***
'Sit down, please,' he said.	***He asked me to sit down.***
'Would you like to sit down?' he said.	***He invited me to sit down.***
'I'd sit down if I was you,' he said.	***He advised me to sit down.***

Reporting verbs we use in this way include:
advise ***ask*** ***invite*** ***order***
remind ***tell*** ***warn***

The normal pattern is **verb + object (+ not) + full infinitive**
The teacher told her students (not) to open their books.
But: we usually don't *invite* or *remind* someone not to do something
we usually only *warn* someone not to do something

There are other reporting verbs which don't follow the pattern of **verb + sb* + full infinitive**. *(In the patterns shown below, *sb* means *'somebody'* and *sth* means *'something'*.) These verbs include:

***accuse* sb* *of* + -ing**
'You stole her bag,' the policeman said to him.
→ *The policeman* ***accused*** *him of stealing her bag.*

admit **+ -ing**
'Yes, I stole her bag,' he said.
→ *He* ***admitted*** *stealing her bag.*

apologise for **+ -ing**
'I'm sorry I stole your bag,' he said to her.
→ *He* ***apologised*** *for stealing her bag.*

deny **+ -ing**
'No, I didn't steal her bag,' he said.
→ *He* ***denied*** *stealing her bag.*

describe **sth* (to sb*)**
'My bag was big and brown,' she said to the policeman.
→ *She* ***described*** *her bag (to the policeman).*

offer **~~sb~~ + full infinitive**
'I'll carry your bag for you,' he said to her.
→ *He* ***offered*** *to carry her bag.*

refuse **~~sb~~ + full infinitive**
'No, I won't give your bag back,' he said to her.
→ *He* ***refused*** *to give her bag back.*

reported questions

We make a statement into a **direct question** by putting a modal, auxiliary or form of *be* before the subject. If the statement does not have a modal, auxiliary or form of *be*, we add *do/does/did* before the subject.
I like shopping. *(Statement)*
Do you like shopping? *(Direct question)*

We can also make a statement into a direct question beginning with a **question word** such as ***What***, ***When***, ***How***, etc. Again, we put a modal, auxiliary or *be* before the subject, and if the statement does not have a modal, auxiliary or *be*, we add *do/does/did* before the subject.
I like buying clothes. *(Statement)*
What do you like buying? *(Direct question)*

A **reported question** begins with a phrase such as *She asked me ...*, and the rest of the reported question goes back to the word order of statements – that is, **subject + modal/ auxiliary** (if there is one) **+ verb**. Notice also that we use backshift, as in reported statements.
She asked me what I liked buying. *(Reported question)*

If the direct question does not begin with a question word, we use the word ***if*** in the reported question. Again, the word order goes back to the word order of statements.
Do you save money regularly? *(Direct question)*
She asked me if I saved money regularly. *(Reported question)*

NATIONAL GEOGRAPHIC LEARNING | CENGAGE Learning

English Explorer Student's Book 4
Helen Stephenson

Publisher: Jason Mann
Commissioning Editor: Alistair Baxter
Assistant Editor: Manuela Barros
Technology Development Manager: Debie Mirtle
Senior Marketing Manager: Ruth McAleavey
Senior Content Project Editor: Natalie Griffith
Production Controller: Denise Power
National Geographic Liaison: Leila Hishmeh
Art Director: Natasa Arsenidou
Cover/Text Designer: Natasa Arsenidou
Compositors: eMC Design Ltd., UK
Audio: EFS Television Production Ltd

Acknowledgements

The publisher would like to thank Robert Crossley for writing the True Story and Project pages.

The Publisher would also like to thank the following for their invaluable contribution: Karen Spiller and Liz Driscoll.

ISBN: 978-1-111-22304-5

National Geographic Learning
Cheriton House, North Way, Andover, Hampshire, SP10 5BE
United Kingdom

Cengage Learning is a leading provider of customized learning solutions with office locations around the globe, including Singapore, the United Kingdom, Australia, Mexico, Brazil and Japan. Locate your local office at: **international.cengage.com/region**

Cengage Learning products are represented in Canada by Nelson Education, Ltd.

Visit National Geographic Learning online at **ngl.cengage.com**
Visit our corporate website at **www.cengage.com**

Photo credits

The publishers would like to thank the following sources for permission to reproduce their copyright protected photographs:

Cover photo: Stephen Alvarez/National Geographic Image Collection

pp 5 (moodboard/Alamy), 6 (Beretta/Sims/Rex Features), 8 (CBS/Landov), 12 (Shutterstock.com), 13c (Shutterstock.com), 13b (Shutterstock.com), 14tl (Philip Ryalls/Redfearns/Getty Images), 14tr (Shutterstock.com), 15 (Vincent J. Musi/National Geographic Image Collection), 16t (Vincent J. Musi/National Geographic Image Collection), 16c (Vincent J. Musi/National Geographic image Collection), 16b (Vincent J. Musi/National Geographic image Collection), 18t (Sodapix/Corbis), 18cl (Peter Knighton/iStockphoto.com), 18cr (Shutterstock.com), 18b (Mike Parry/Minden Pictures/National Geographic Image Collection), 22 (Shutterstock.com), 24cr (Shutterstock.com), 24bl (Beverly Joubert/National Geographic Image Collection), 24br (aleksandrovaphoto/iStockphoto.com), 29 (Shutterstock.com), 30 (International Mammoth Committee/National Geographic Image Collection), 32mr (William Gottlieb/Corbis), 32br (Acik/Bigstockphoto.com), 33bl (Ian Shaw/Alamy), 33 inset (Hulton Archive/Getty Images), 35 (Alistair Wilson 50/50/PA Archive/Press Association Images), 36 (morganl/iStockphoto.com), 37 (Science Museum of Brussels/wikipedia.com), 38t (Shutterstock.com), 38 inset (Shutterstock.com), 39 (lagereek/iStockphoto.com), 40tr (Clive Rose/Getty Images), 40cr (Fred DuFour/Getty Images), 43tl (LajosRepasi/iStockphoto.com), 43tcl (iconogenic/iStockphoto.com), 43bcl (dsteller/iStockphoto.com), 43bl (123foto/iStockphoto.com), 43c (quix429/iStockphoto.com), 43r (iconogenic/iStockphoto.com), 46mr (Filippo Monteforte/Getty Images), 46bl (Maliketh/iStockphoto.com), 46br (Shutterstock.com), 47 (Richard Heathcote/Staff), 52tr (Shutterstock.com), 52cr (Shutterstock.com), 42br (Shutterstock.com), 53 (Atlantide Phototravel/Corbis), 54t (vodkamax/iStockphoto.com), 54c (Mike Theiss/National Geographic Image Collection), 55 (Shutterstock.com), 56 (Robert Clark/National Geographic Image Collection), 59 (Shutterstock.com), 60c (Peter Essick/National Geographic Image Collection), 60b (Peter Essick/National Geographic Image Collection), 61tl (Shutterstock.com), 61tr (npix/iStockphoto.com), 61bl (Shutterstock.com), 61br (Denis/Fotolia.com), 62bg (Shutterstock.com), 62tr (Shutterstock.com), 62bl (Shutterstock.com), 62br (Shutterstock.com), 63 (Albright-Knox Art Gallery/Corbis), 64 inset (Black Dog & Leventhal), 64bg (Shutterstock.com), 66 (Pojbic/iStockphoto.com), 70–71bg (anneleven/iStockphoto.com), 70bl (Houghton Mifflin Harcourt), 70bc (Theodore Von Holst (1810–1844)/wikipedia.com), 70br (Chicago: National Prtg. & Engr. Co.), 71t (ivan-96/iStockphoto.com), 71b (Alinari Archives/Corbis), 76 (The Art Archive/Tate Gallery London/Eileen Tweedy), 77 (Mark Thiessen/National Geographic Image Collection), 78r (Ian Miles, Flashpoint Pictures/Alamy), 78l (Shutterstock.com), 80 (Tim Rooke/Rex Features), 81l (Topical Press Agency/Stringer/Getty Images), 81cl (Fox Photos/Getty Images), 81cr (Joseph Scherschel/Getty Images), 81r (Laruffa/Rex Features), 84t (Volkmar K. Wentzel/National Geographic Image Collection), 84c (MogensTrolle/iStockphoto.com), 84b (gregul/iStockphoto.com), 86t (Andrew Brusso/Corbis), 86c (Shutterstock.com), 87 (Susan Barr/Getty Images), 88l (© Starbucks), 88r (Fair Trade Resource Network), 90bl (Jeff Greenberg/Alamy), 90bc (77studio/iStockphoto.com), 90br (RubberBall/Alamy), 94l (eddie tor/Fotolia.com), 94–95bl (Bestway Inflatables), 95br (Images Scientific Instruments Inc), 108 (Shutterstock.com), 109 (Shutterstock.com), 110 (Shutterstock.com), 111 (Shutterstock.com), 112 (Shutterstock.com), 113 (Shutterstock.com), 114 (Shutterstock.com), 115 (Shutterstock.com)

The following photographs were taken on commission © Heinle, Cengage Learning by MM Studios Ltd. pp 4, 10, 20, 34, 44, 58, 68, 82, 92. The publisher would like to thank the following for their help with the location photography: St Gregory the Great School, Oxford; Blackwell Bookshop Oxford; HMV, Oxford.

Illustrations by Celia Hart pp 7, 31, 32, 50, 57, 74, 85, 98, 101, 102, 104; Janos Jantner (Beehive Illustration) pp 26, 65, 97, 100, 106; Norbert Sipos (Beehive Illustration) p 93; Eric Smith pp 17, 41, 49, 73, 79, 83, 89, 103

Printed in China by RR Donnelley
Print Number: 06 Print Year: 2016